RONALD ANNO

WALL STREET
and
YOUR RETIREMENT

*WHAT THE BULLS AND BEARS
DON'T WANT YOU TO KNOW*

Copyright © 2020 by Ronald Anno.

All rights reserved. No part of this publication may be reproduced, distributed, or transmitted in any form or by any means, including photocopying, recording, or other electronic or mechanical methods, without the prior written permission of the publisher, except in the case of brief quotations embodied in critical reviews and certain other noncommercial uses permitted by copyright law. For permission requests, write to the publisher at the address below. These materials are provided to you by Ron Anno for informational purposes only and Ron Anno and Advisors Excel, LLC expressly disclaim any and all liability arising out of or relating to your use of same. The provision of these materials does not constitute legal or investment advice and does not establish an attorney-client relationship between you and Ron Anno. No tax advice is contained in these materials. You are solely responsible for ensuring the accuracy and completeness of all materials as well as the compliance, validity, and enforceability of all materials under any applicable law. The advice and strategies found within may not be suitable for every situation. You are expressly advised to consult with a qualified attorney or other professional in making any such determination and to determine your legal or financial needs. No warranty of any kind, implied, expressed, or statutory, including but not limited to the warranties of title and non-infringement of third-party rights, is given with respect to this publication.

Retirement Planning & Investment Solutions LLC
37 S. Indiana Ave., Suite 103, Englewood, FL 34223
941.615.0077

Book layout ©2020 Advisors Excel, LLC

Wall Street & Your Retirement/Ronald Anno—1st edition

ISBN 9798667121435

Investment advisory services offered only by duly registered individuals through AE Wealth Management, LLC (AEWM). AEWM and Retirement Planning and Investment Solutions LLC are not affiliated companies.

Investing involves risk, including the potential loss of principal. No investment strategy can guarantee a profit or protect against loss in periods of declining values. None of the information contained in this book shall constitute an offer to sell or solicit any offer to buy a security or any insurance product.

Safe Money Financial Solutions LLC is our name and it does not promise or guarantee investment results or preservation of principal. Any references to protection benefits, safety, security, or steady and reliable income streams on this website refer only to fixed insurance products. They do not refer, in any way, to securities or investment advisory products. Annuity guarantees are backed by the financial strength and claims-paying ability of the issuing insurance company. Annuities are insurance products that may be subject to fees, surrender charges and holding periods which vary by insurance company. Annuities are not FDIC insured.

The strategies outlined in this book may not be suitable for every individual and are not guaranteed or warranted to produce any particular results. Presentation of performance data herein does not imply that similar results will be achieved in the future. Any such data are provided merely for illustrative and discussion purposes.

Investing involves risk, including the potential loss of principal. No investment strategy can guarantee a profit or protect against loss in periods of declining values. Insurance products and annuities are guaranteed by the insurance companies themselves. The guarantees offered by these products are dependent on the claims-paying ability of the insurance companies.

The contents of this book are provided for informational purposes only and are not intended to serve as the basis for any financial decisions. Any tax, legal or estate planning information is general in nature. It should not be construed as legal or tax advice. Always consult an attorney or tax professional regarding the applicability of this information to your unique situation.

What Professionals Are Saying About *Wall Street and Your Retirement*

"Ron Anno's *Wall Street and Your Retirement* takes the complex and multi-faceted process of retirement planning and breaks it down into its components in a way that is comprehensible to those without specialized financial knowledge. His descriptions of the various elements that compose a retirement plan are concise and free of unnecessary industry jargon or niche phrases. His examples of how these individual parts work together to form a greater whole is direct and unambiguous in underscoring the importance of having a financial professional with diversified knowledge planning for your retirement goals."
Paul J. Bupivi, Esq.
Lawrence & Associates—Counselors at Law

"Retirement planning is crucial for almost everyone. Yet, most of us do not understand how to set up a diversified plan that will meet our retirement goals or, in some cases, what our goals even are. Ron's book provides valuable insight into forming an effective retirement plan. It discusses all aspects of a truly diverse retirement plan, from identifying retirement goals to explaining the various tools and products available and showing how each can be used in a solid retirement plan. Ron explains the roles that health care, the stock market, annuities, life insurance, Social Security, and estate planning each play in retirement. My favorite aspect of this book is that it provides an understanding of how different types of complex annuities and life insurance policies actually work. This book is worth reading for that alone but it provides much more to help the reader gain a better understanding of retirement planning."
Robert C. Benedict, Esq.
Wideikis, Benedict & Berntsson, LLC
The Big W Law Firm

*Set your goals wisely,
pursue them intelligently,
and you'll make your mark.*

~ Roger A. Durant

Table of Contents

The Importance of Planning i
    Diversified Portfolio vs. Diversified Strategies iii
A Random Walk Down Wall Street 1
    How the Animal-Broker Craze Began 2
Riddle Me This? 7
How to Create a Financial Plan 15
Taxes 19
    The Fed 20
    Know Your Limits 21
    Assuming a Lower Tax Rate 22
    401(k)/IRA 22
Market Volatility 25
    The Color of Money 26
    Dollar-Cost Averaging 28
    Is There a "Perfect" Product? 29
Retirement Income 31
    Sources of Income 32
    Retirement Income Needs 35
    Other Expenses 38
    Putting It All Together 42
Longevity 47

    Retiring Later 49
    Health Care 50
    Long-Term Care 51
    Long-Term and Home Health Care 59
    Spousal Planning 63

Social Security 65
    The Future of Social Security 65
    Full Retirement Age 68
    Spousal Benefits 72
    Taxes, Taxes, Taxes 75
    Working and Social Security: The Earnings Test 77

401(k)s & IRAs 79
    RMDs 84
    Roth 86
    Taking Charge 86

Annuities 89
    How You Get Paid 90
    Types of Annuities 92
    Other Things to Know About Annuities 95

Estate & Legacy 97
    Documents 98
    Taxes 103

Indexed Universal Life 105
    Insurance: The Basics 105
    Permanent Insurance 106
    INDEXING 109

2020 and Beyond 115
Acknowledgments 119
About the Author 121

FOREWORD
The Importance of Planning

We are all shaped by the events in our lives. Most of us have a few defined events that forever change our stories, who we are, and the choices we make. The story of my event begins in January of 1973. My grandparents, Otto and Jenny, had agreed to raise my brother and me at the ages of nine and ten, respectively. They had just retired to a little town called Largo in Florida. In addition to the two of us, they were responsible for my uncle, who had special needs. My parents were going through a divorce, and in the midst of this chaos, I was excited and grateful to be in our little two-bedroom, two-bath house. My brother and I slept in the Florida room.

My grandfather would be receiving his first Social Security income and retirement check at the end of the month. It was at this time, he received a call that I remember vividly. He learned his $400 monthly retirement check was going to be less than $40. My grandfather owned a butcher shop in Chicago and paid $40 every two weeks into a special program. That's $80 per month for nearly twenty years. When the union asked him for receipts of these payments, he couldn't provide them—he had paid directly out of the cash register to an intermediary, a man he had trusted.

My grandfather's first Social Security income check was about $180. With his other retirement funds at less than a tenth of what he expected, Otto learned he would be supporting our family of five on about $220 a month. When the news settled in, my grandmother asked, "Are we going to be okay?" Their voices lowered and I never heard the rest of the conversation.

My grandfather was a great man. He would look you in the eyes, shake your hand, and stand by his word. Not everyone lives by the same principles. In time, my grandparents made friends. They played cards on Fridays and Sundays in the kitchen. I would sit on the floor playing with my toy cars and listen to the old people talk. They couldn't believe people were living to be as old as seventy-five. I remember Mr. Buscher saying he had found someone in the obituaries section who died at the age of eighty. The biggest concern my grandparents' friends had was whether they would have enough money to live, if they lived that long. To this day, I believe their greatest fear was ending up like my grandparents.

What can you learn from my family's story? What would Otto and Jenny advise you to do in retirement? I think the first thing Jenny would tell you is to ask the question, "Are we going to be okay?" *before* an unexpected event takes place. She would advise you to have your spouse explain why and how you will be secure in retirement. My grandfather would probably tell you a paycheck or consistent income is just as important when you retire as when you are working. It doesn't matter if it was forty-seven years ago or today. Retirees have the same concern of having enough money to live on, and being able to answer the question of whether they will outlive their money.

The author's grandparents.

You may be curious as to what my grandfather did to keep everything together. He knocked on doors to find work. He found two opportunities for work and took both. He worked until the day he died! Out of respect and love for Otto and Jenny, part of my mission is to educate others so they don't make the same mistakes.

Diversified Portfolio vs. Diversified Strategies

I don't mind playing the game if I understand the rules, and, in my opinion, Rule No. 1 is this: In retirement, expect the unexpected. Having a nest egg is important.

Often, people talk about diversification—not having all of your eggs in one basket. Unfortunately, we often see people who have taken that to mean different stock categories, different investment allocations. These are important, of course, but that's a little like having different kind of eggs still in the same basket—the Wall Street basket. If the basket tips over, all of the eggs in it are still at risk.

This is why it's important that you work with someone who will represent your best interests in regard to your financial plans. You want to work with people who understand that you don't just need diversification in one basket; you need multiple baskets. This is the difference between a diversified portfolio and a plan that has diversified strategies, and different ways of using several baskets to your best advantage. Having a written plan that spells out what you have, where you have it, how it's coordinated, and how all of your money is working together for your good is one way to address the kinds of problems Jenny and Otto faced.

Regardless of whether you are already retired or approaching retirement, most people are looking for peace of mind. Peace of mind cannot be achieved without clarity of your personal financial situation. A written income plan is your personal road map to your future.

CHAPTER 1

A Random Walk Down Wall Street

What you are about to read is true. I am about to tell you a few stories that aren't commonly known about successful investors.

One of these stories is about Raven. Raven never attended Harvard or Yale. She had no formal training on Wall Street or in Chicago. Raven was very unique and had a very specific set of skills. In 1999, she outperformed more than 6,000 professional brokers during the stock market rally with a 213 percent return. She quadrupled the performance of the Dow and doubled the performance of the NASDAQ.[1] Raven was so successful and became so recognized an index was named in her honor. In fact, Raven, with no formal investment training, is in the Guinness Book of World Records as she was the twenty-second most successful money manager of the year in the U.S.

Raven has also been recognized in the Guinness Book of World Records as the most successful chimp on Wall Street. [2]

---

[1] Bloomberg. January 8, 1999. "Internet Stock Review Announces MonkeyDex." https://www.bloomberg.com/press-releases/1999-01-08/internet-stock-review-announces-monkeydex

[2] Guinness Book of World Records. "Most Successful Chimpanzee on Wall Street." https://www.guinnessworldrecords.com/world-records/most-successful-chimpanzee-on-wall-street?fb_comment_id=857479987607045_1773344436020591

Wait . . . what? Raven is an animal? Yes!

Like an ape? Yes!

You mean a monkey? Yes . . . Raven is a chimp.

In fact, Raven has a lot of friends, other monkeys who successfully received better returns than some nationally recognized money managers, hedge fund managers, and stockbrokers. After much discussion, it was decided that the monkeys had an uncompetitive edge, so they blindfolded some monkeys prior to the investment choices. And what was the result? The blindfolded monkeys won! In fact, Orlando the Cat has been a winner![3] A stock-pickin' chicken . . . you guessed it, a true champ! [4]

And if you're wondering how Raven and other primates made these investment decisions, it was by throwing darts at a list of stocks attached to a dart board. That's how they chose investments that performed better than some well-known, highly educated, and experienced brokers and managers.

At the end of this chapter, I will disclose why it's important for you to understand this information. And if you're still wondering about the name of the index that was given to Raven in her honor, it's called MonkeyDex.

And just as everything you will read is absolutely true, so are the following stories, to name a few.

How the Animal-Broker Craze Began

Burton Malkiel is a well-respected Princeton University professor, economist and writer who wrote a book called *A Random Walk Down Wall Street*.

---

[3] Mark King. The Observer. January 13, 2013. "Investments: Orlando is the Cat's Whiskers of Investing."
https://www.theguardian.com/money/2013/jan/13/investments-stock-picking

[4] William S. Rukeyser. CNN Money. September 27, 1996. "This Chicken Can Pick 'Em."
https://money.cnn.com/1996/09/27/personalfinance/yomo_worst/

In his 1973 bestselling book he proclaimed:
"A blindfolded monkey throwing darts at a newspaper's financial pages could select a portfolio that would do just as well as one carefully selected by experts."

Over the years, many professional money managers and experts have put Mr. Malkiel's theory to the test.

One of those individuals was Rob Arnott, CEO of Research Affiliates. A column by Rick Ferri in *Forbes* highlights Arnott's research from the simulated results of a hundred monkeys throwing darts at the stock pages of the newspaper, which revealed that the "monkey picks" would outperform the index.

"'Malkiel was wrong,' stated Arnott at the IMN Global Indexing and ETFs conference. 'The monkeys have done a much better job than both the experts and the stock market.'

"The average monkey outperformed the index by 1.7 percent per year since 1964. That's a lot of bananas!" [5]

Orlando the House Cat

A story in the British newspaper, *The Observer,* the financial-oriented pages of *The Guardian,* generated a lot of buzz at the end of 2012. It details the result of a little experiment the paper ran in 2012, where it gave the same imaginary amount, £5,000, to some professional money managers, some children aged eleven to eighteen, and a ginger tabby cat. The three groups were told to make trades each quarter through the year on any stocks in the FTSE All-Share Index.

Partway through the year, all hypothetical portfolio values had increased, but the professionals were in the lead. By quarter four, a few final trades put the professionals in second place, the students were in third (although they had the best quarter of all in Q4), and Orlando the cat took first. The tabby

---

[5] Rick Ferri. Forbes. December 20, 2012. "Any Monkey Can Beat the Market." https://www.forbes.com/sites/rickferri/2012/12/20/any-monkey-can-beat-the-market/#2024cb6b630a

earned 10 percent more than the professional money managers with his picks. How?

"While the professionals used their decades of investment knowledge and traditional stock-picking methods, the cat selected stocks by throwing his favorite toy mouse on a grid of numbers allocated to different companies."

Unfortunately, there were no professional words of advice from Orlando about how to repeat his outstanding success.

"A spokeswoman for Orlando said he was not available to give an interview because of a claws in his contract."[6]

Bird Brain the Stock-Pickin' Chicken

"This chicken can pick 'em"

That was the title of a leading financial story back in 1996.

CNN made its own market index based on "Bird Brain, the Stock Pickin' Chicken." The team would lay out newspaper financial pages, and, as the chicken pecked around, the CNN newsies would note where he pecked and include those companies as the chicken's stock picks.

The S&P 500 Index is a measurement of 500 large cap companies' stocks across broad swaths of industry, and is frequently referenced as a stable, fairly accurate measure of the American economy. For the year from June 13, 1995, to June 13, 1996, Bird Brain's picks rose 19 percent, while the S&P 500 rose 24.6 percent. So, Bird Brain's picks weren't quite market leaders.

However, there were other indexes and indexed funds that Bird Brain *did* outperform—by quite a lot. For instance, Steadman Technology & Growth Funds posted a 17 percent *loss* for the same time period.

---

[6] Mark King. *The Observer*. January 13, 2013. "Investments: Orlando is the Cat's Whiskers of Investing."
https://www.theguardian.com/money/2013/jan/13/investments-stock-picking

"The people that are still in (the Steadman funds) just are totally unaware," Sheldon Jacobs, editor of *No-Load Fund Investor,* said. "They are not following their investments, and that's the first rule of investing—to follow it."

According to the CNN article about Bird Brain's success, the Steadman funds had fees of more than 16 percent. By comparison, CNN's Bird Brain had reasonable returns and worked just on the cost of birdseed and water.[7]

So why are those stories so important to consider? The very people who are giving you investment advice on how to prepare for retirement might not be able to outperform barnyard animals and household pets in a side by side contest.

This isn't to say you shouldn't get investing advice. It is, however, to say that any advice that circles around beating the market, getting fantastic returns, or never-fail stock picks is not sound advice at all. It's more like taking your money to the race track or roulette table. If you're looking for sound strategies that will take you—and your money—the distance, and support your lifestyle through retirement, you need advice that is in your best interests, that takes a long view, and that encompasses all aspects of your financial life.

As a former stockbroker and principal/owner of a stock brokerage firm in downtown Chicago, I can say firsthand I think much of the advice given today is not in your best interest.

Preparing for retirement is much more complex than simply picking some stock winners. You have Social Security, income, Medicare costs, and taxation issues just to name a few, which all need careful consideration before you make any decisions. Complicating matters, many of these decisions give you one opportunity to make the right choice.

How do you find the professional help and guidance you need? For a start, I suggest that you look for someone who has

---

7 William S. Rukeyser. CNN Money. September 27, 1996. "This Chicken Can Pick 'Em."
https://money.cnn.com/1996/09/27/personalfinance/yomo_worst/

a fiduciary duty, as opposed to just a stockbroker or an insurance agent. A fiduciary is required to represent your best interest and not the brokerage house or insurance company. Your stockbroker may be your best friend or even a relative, but they are only allowed to represent what the brokerage house allows them to sell you.

The next few chapters of this book will identify some problems with common theories often suggested during retirement and then potential solutions to these problems will be presented.

When I deal with clients and as I write this book I am striving to be as perfect as I can in an imperfect environment.

My hope for you after reading this information is that it provides you a clearer path to success or that at least it prompts you to ask questions you may otherwise not have thought to ask.

At some point in time, I will also retire and will make decisions that will impact my family's financial wellbeing. After being in the business nearly thirty-five years and knowing the business as well as I do, I am keenly aware of the importance of these choices. They aren't always easy decisions to make. I don't know about you, but I'd prefer not having to resort to a stock pickin' chicken or an award-winning monkey.

CHAPTER 2

Riddle Me This?

P eter and Polly retire at age sixty-five, each with a retirement portfolio of $250,000. Both withdraw the exact same amount of $12,500 every year. At the end of sixteen years, both have withdrawn a total of $200,000. How is it that Polly has a portfolio balance of $288,120 and Peter only has $19,009? (Answer on the next page.)

This story is about "Sequence of Returns Risk." This is the risk of retiring in a bear market. If you withdraw money to live on or take RMDs as the market is going down, this could lead to reducing your retirement savings prematurely.

According to a piece in *Kiplinger Magazine*, from 1926 to 2017, bull markets have historically lasted an average of nine years. A typical bear market has lasted 1.4 years with an average loss of 41 percent.[8] Of course, our bull market run of 2010s lasted over a decade but we have certainly cooled off as the international coronavirus pandemic sets off volatility. As of this writing, no one knows if this is the beginning of a longer bear cycle, or whether this is a rocky bump in the road. What I *know* is, whether you have an IRA, 401(k) or other retirement account, the IRS requires you to begin to take distributions beginning at age seventy-two. Those distributions are mandatory whether or not the stock market is running up in a

---

[8] First Trust as referenced by Michael Alloi. *Kiplinger*. March 23, 2018. https://www.kiplinger.com/article/retirement/T037-C032-S014-the-biggest-risk-retirees-face-right-now.html

bull market or declining in a bear market. During a bear market, when asset values are declining, the same distribution amount required by the IRS is a higher percentage of the total account balance than when asset values are increasing. As you age, your RMD percentage increases. If you choose not to take an RMD, the tax penalties could be as high as 50 percent of the amount you should have taken out. This is something that both Polly and Peter will have to encounter in their retirements, as demonstrated in the following example.

> *Polly retired in December 1995 and Peter retired in December 1999. Polly retired in a bull market. Peter retired at the beginning of a bear market. Quite often the quality of retirement is based upon luck and timing.*

Peter

$250,000 invested in S&P 500-like fund, December 1999 to December 2018, with 5% annual withdrawal

Year	Beginning Value	Index Return	Account Change	Annual Withdrawal
1999	$250,000	-10.14%	-$25,350	$12,500
2000	$212,150	-13.03%	-$27,643	$12,500
2001	$172,007	-23.34%	-$40,146	$12,500
2002	$119,360	26.36%	$31,463	$12,500
2003	$138,324	8.99%	$12,435	$12,500
2004	$138,259	2.97%	$4,106	$12,500
2005	$129,865	13.62%	$17,688	$12,500
2006	$135,053	3.53%	$4,767	$12,500
2007	$127,321	-38.49%	-$49,006	$12,500
2008	$65,815	23.48%	$15,453	$12,500
2009	$68,768	12.83%	$8,823	$12,500
2010	$65,091	0.00%	$0	$12,500
2011	$52,591	13.35%	$7,021	$12,500
2012	$47,112	29.59%	$13,940	$12,500
2013	$48,553	11.36%	$5,516	$12,500
2014	$41,568	-0.73%	-$303	$12,500
2015	$28,765	9.54%	$2,744	$12,500
2016	$19,009	19.44%	$3,695	$12,500
2017	$10,204	-6.25%	-$638	$12,500
2018	-$2,934			
	Total Change in Account Value: -101.17%			

Polly

\$250,000 invested in S&P 500-like fund, December 1995 to December 2018, with 5% annual withdrawal			
Year	Beginning Value	Index Return	Account Change	Annual Withdrawal
1995	$250,000	20.29%	$50,725	$12,500
1996	$288,225	30.90%	$89,062	$12,500
1997	$364,787	26.70%	$97,398	$12,500
1998	$449,685	19.53%	$87,823	$12,500
1999	$525,008	-10.14%	-$53,236	$12,500
2000	$459,272	-13.03%	-$59,843	$12,500
2001	$386,929	-23.34%	-$90,309	$12,500
2002	$284,120	26.36%	$74,894	$12,500
2003	$346,514	8.99%	$31,152	$12,500
2004	$365,165	2.97%	$10,845	$12,500
2005	$363,511	13.62%	$49,510	$12,500
2006	$400,521	3.53%	$14,138	$12,500
2007	$402,159	-38.49%	-$154,791	$12,500
2008	$234,868	23.48%	$55,147	$12,500
2009	$277,515	12.83%	$35,605	$12,500
2010	$300,620	0.00%	$0	$12,500
2011	$288,120	13.35%	$38,464	$12,500
2012	$314,084	29.59%	$92,938	$12,500
2013	$394,522	11.36%	$44,818	$12,500
2014	$426,840	-0.73%	-$3,116	$12,500
2015	$411,224	9.54%	$39,231	$12,500
2016	$437,955	19.44%	$85,138	$12,500
2017	$510,593	-6.25%	-$31,912	$12,500
2018	$466,181			
	Total Change in Account Value: 86.47%			

In the previous illustrations, Peter runs out of money by the end of 2017 and Polly has more than $460,000 remaining. Now, these illustrations do not reflect taxes or advisor fees and are hypothetical and only represent past performance. While no one can predict what the market will do in the future, this demonstrates that planning and proper timing is crucial in determining when to retire. Notice also the prior two illustrations keep the income of Polly and Peter set at $12,500 a year. This is hardly realistic: Inflation would eat away at their purchasing power.

For the next example, let's increase the annual withdrawal by 2 percent, to keep up with the cost of living and inflation. You'll see the more income the two must withdraw from their portfolios, the results are even more dramatic, as the next two illustrations reflect.

You'll see that, in the following illustrations, by increasing the annual withdrawal by just two percent, Peter, who unluckily began his retirement in December of 1999, is out of money by 2013. Polly, however, will begin 2018 going strong, having withdrawn $19,324 in 2017 with a remaining principal balance of nearly $350,000.

Peter

$250,000 invested in S&P 500-like fund, December 1999 to December 2018, with 5% annual withdrawal increased 2% per year to address inflation

Year	Beginning Value	Index Return	Account Change	Annual Withdrawal
1999	$250,000	-10.14%	-$25,350	$12,500
2000	$212,150	-13.03%	-$27,643	$12,750
2001	$171,757	-23.34%	-$40,088	$13,005
2002	$118,664	26.36%	$31,280	$13,265
2003	$136,678	8.99%	$12,287	$13,530
2004	$135,435	2.97%	$4,022	$13,801
2005	$125,657	13.62%	$17,114	$14,077
2006	$128,694	3.53%	$4,543	$14,359
2007	$118,879	-38.49%	-$45,756	$14,646
2008	$58,477	23.48%	$13,730	$14,939
2009	$57,268	12.83%	$7,348	$15,237
2010	$49,378	0.00%	$0	$15,542
2011	$33,836	13.35%	$4,517	$15,853
2012	$22,500	29.59%	$6,658	$16,170
2013	$12,988	11.36%	$1,475	$16,493
2014	-$2,030	-0.73%	$15	$16,823
2015	-$18,839	9.54%	-$1,797	$17,160
2016	-$37,796	19.44%	-$7,347	$17,503
2017	-$62,646	-6.25%	$3,915	$17,853
2018	-$76,584			
	Total Change in Account Value: -130.64%			

Polly

$250,000 invested in S&P 500-like fund, December 1995 to December 2018, with 5% annual withdrawal and 2% annual increase to address inflation

Year	Beginning Value	Index Return	Account Change	Annual Withdrawal
1995	$250,000	20.29%	$50,725	$12,500
1996	$288,225	30.90%	$89,062	$12,750
1997	$364,537	26.70%	$97,331	$13,005
1998	$448,863	19.53%	$87,663	$13,265
1999	$523,261	-10.14%	-$53,059	$13,530
2000	$456,672	-13.03%	-$59,504	$13,801
2001	$383,366	-23.34%	-$89,478	$14,077
2002	$279,812	26.36%	$73,758	$14,359
2003	$339,211	8.99%	$30,495	$14,646
2004	$355,061	2.97%	$10,545	$14,939
2005	$350,667	13.62%	$47,761	$15,237
2006	$383,191	3.53%	$13,527	$15,542
2007	$381,175	-38.49%	-$146,714	$15,853
2008	$218,608	23.48%	$51,329	$16,170
2009	$253,767	12.83%	$32,558	$16,493
2010	$269,832	0.00%	$0	$16,823
2011	$253,008	13.35%	$33,777	$17,160
2012	$269,625	29.59%	$79,782	$17,503
2013	$331,904	11.36%	$37,704	$17,853
2014	$351,755	-0.73%	-$2,568	$18,210
2015	$330,977	9.54%	$31,575	$18,574
2016	$343,978	19.44%	$66,869	$18,946
2017	$391,902	-6.25%	-$24,494	$19,325
2018	$348,083			
	Total Change in Account Value: 39.23%			

CHAPTER 3

How to Create a Financial Plan

Creating a financial plan is important because you are mapping out your retirement future. If you are a pre-retiree or currently in retirement not having a plan might just be comparable to hopping on a plane not knowing if you have enough fuel to get to your final destination. Let's talk about how some people develop a plan.

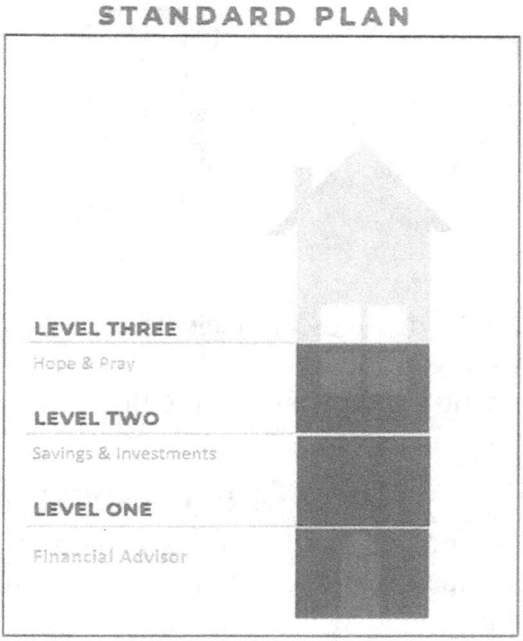

Step 1: Find a financial advisor or stockbroker.

Step 2: Hand over your savings and investments.

Step 3: Hope and pray. It took you forty years to accumulate those monies and you don't want to lose your savings in a year or two.

STANDARD PLAN

LEVEL THREE
Hope & Pray

LEVEL TWO
Savings & Investments

LEVEL ONE
Financial Advisor

Hoping and praying are good things. A hope-and-pray investment plan is not.

The following is a plan I developed:

F.R.E.S.H. Start Plan

A retirement plan is strategic. The foundation of the plan is about defining your dream. Let me ask you a few questions:

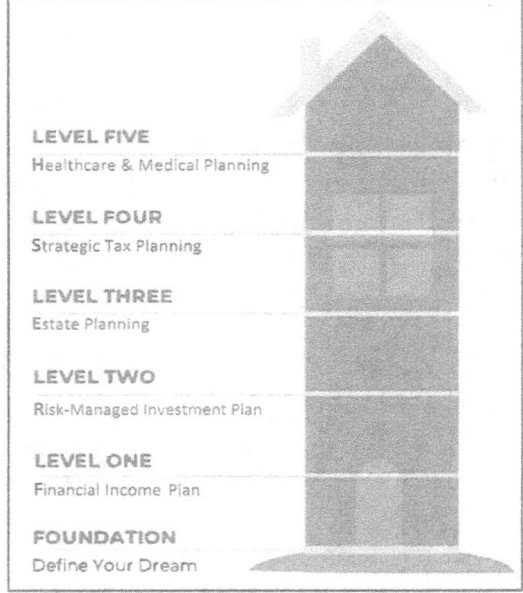

- What does one perfect day in your life look like?
- Where are you at?
- Who are you with?
- What are you doing?
- How do you feel at the end of the day?

Your goal during retirement is to take your perfect day and re-create it into many days or weeks and if possible, months. If you put your focus on your personal dream, then your financial decisions can become much easier for you. After you have defined your dream, the next step or level is having a Financial Income Plan.

Level One: Financial Income Plan

Income is a key to having a successful retirement. You had a paycheck while you were working. A paycheck or paychecks can help you live in retirement because it provides a constant income stream.

Level Two: <u>R</u>isk Managed Investment Plan

When you are invested in the market, you have exposure to market risk. The old saying is, "without risk you can have no reward." I represent a Registered Investment Adviser that has an agreement with Sterling Capital Management. Sterling manages the portfolios of some of the largest companies in the world. Companies such as Apple, Amazon, Facebook, and Calpers, just to name a few. Why would these companies choose Sterling Capital to manage their portfolios? There's no conflict of interest. No conflict of interest means they receive no extra compensation or participate in any revenue sharing agreements with mutual funds or other money managers. They place their clients' interests ahead of their own interest. A Risk Managed Investment Plan makes sure you are not taking unnecessary chances with your money and not paying unnecessary fees.

Level Three: <u>E</u>state Planning

Estate planning is making sure your loved ones get what you want them to have at the appropriate time within their lives. Here is a typical conversation: "Ron, I love my child. They're bright, brilliant, and beautiful, they just make bad choices in life." An estate plan could work well for folks who find themselves in a similar situation in which they want to protect their kids from themselves. Although I do not provide legal advice, here are three misunderstandings I have frequently observed in trusts for residents of Florida:

    1. Houses placed in trusts need to be titled in the name of the trustee. Houses are not to be titled in the name of the trust.

    2. Trusts are not creditor proof and do not insulate you from lawsuits.

    3. In most circumstances, it's best not to make your trust the beneficiary of your IRA or 401(k).

Level Four: Strategic Tax Planning

In my opinion, many people pay too much in taxes unknowingly and unnecessarily. The next several years can offer an opportunity to take taxable IRAs and convert them into non-taxable accounts, if it makes sense for your situation. Why would you want to consider this option? Because tax rates will revert back to the original tax tables on December 31, 2025 unless Congress passes an extension to continue these lower rates. The timing of when to turn on Social Security, draw monies out of IRA's and non-qualified accounts is crucial. For example, withdrawing 5 percent out of your IRA coupled with a market correction could alter your retirement plans significantly. A strategic tax plan is imperative during retirement.

Level Five: Health Care & Medical Planning

When you retire, health care expenses will probably be your biggest expense next to taxes. Ten thousand people a day are turning sixty-five, qualifying for Medicare for the next fifteen years. The majority of Medicare costs, Parts B & D, are being subsidized by the federal government. With the volume of baby boomers turning sixty-five every day, the Medicare trustees have stated those costs will be passed back to those who can afford it most. With new changes being implemented, up to 90 percent of the cost of Medicare Parts B & D will now be the responsibility of "those who can afford it most."[9] The types of income you have and timing of distributions are imperative during retirement.

---

[9] Budget of the U.S. Government Fiscal year 2014 - pg. 38

CHAPTER 4
Taxes

Where to begin with taxes? Perhaps by acknowledging we all bear responsibility for the resources we share. Roads, bridges, schools ... It is the patriotic duty of every American to pay his or her fair share of taxes. Many would agree with me, though, that while they don't mind paying their fair share, they're not interested in paying one cent more!

Now, just talking taxes probably takes your mind to April, tax season. You are probably thinking about all the forms you collect and how you file. Perhaps you are thinking about your certified public accountant or another qualified tax professional and saying to yourself, "I've already got taxes taken care of, thanks!"

However, what I see when people come into my office is that their relationship with their tax professional is purely a January through April relationship. That means they may have a tax professional, but not a tax *planner*.

What I mean by that is tax planning extends beyond filing taxes. In April, we are required to do an accounting with the IRS to make sure we have paid up on our bill or to settle the score if we have overpaid. But real tax planning is about making each financial move in a way that allows you to keep the most money in your pocket and out of Uncle Sam's.

Now, as a caveat, I want to emphasize that I am not a CPA, nor am I a tax planner, but I see the way taxes affect my clients, and I have plenty of experience helping clients with tax-efficient strategies in their retirement income plans, in conjunction with their tax professionals.

It is especially important to me to help my clients develop tax-efficient strategies in their retirement income plans because each dollar they can keep in their pockets is a dollar we can put to work.

Tax professionals prepare and report your previous year's earning history. I help my clients prepare in advance for this event. When I work with a client, the ideal plan preparation involves the clients' tax professional's participation because I want you to have the assurance that it not only meets your approval but has the blessing of your certified public accountant. In other words, I want to make sure your financial plan is complimentary to your tax plan. Having qualified financial, tax, and legal professionals in your corner working together for your benefit is an ideal solution.

The Fed

Now, in the United States, taxes can be a rather uncertain proposition. Currently, with a Republican-controlled Congress and an Administration that places a hefty emphasis on protecting personal property rights, it would be easy to assume tax rates could decline in the next four to eight years. However, there is one (large!) factor that we, as a nation, must confront: the national debt.

Currently, according to USDebtClock.org, we are over $20,000,000,000,000 in debt and climbing. That's $20 TRILLION with a T. With just $1 trillion, you could park it in the bank at a zero percent interest rate and still spend more than $54 million every day for fifty years without hitting a zero balance.

Even if Congress got a handle and stopped that debt from its daily compound, divided by each taxpayer, we each would owe about $175,000. So, will that be check or cash?

My point here isn't to give you anxiety. I'm just saying, even with the rosiest of outlooks on our personal income tax rates, you cannot count on low tax rates for the long term. Instead, you and your network of professionals (tax, legal and financial) should constantly be looking for ways to take advantage of tax-saving opportunities as they come. After all, the best "luck" is when proper planning meets opportunity.

So, how can we get started?

Know Your Limits

One of the foundational pieces of tax planning is knowing what tax bracket you are in based on your income after removing pre-tax or untaxed assets. Your income taxes are based on everything on which you have to pay taxes.

One reason to know your income tax rate is so you can see how far away you are from the next lower or higher tax bracket. This is particularly important when it comes to decisions such as gifting and Roth IRA rollovers. You will want to be sure to talk to a tax professional and a financial advisor qualified to provide investment advice prior to making any decisions.

For instance, based on the 2020 tax table, Mallory and Ralph's taxable income is just over $330,000, putting them in the 32 percent tax bracket and about $3,400 above the upper end of the 24 percent tax bracket. They have already maxed out their retirement funds' tax-exempt contributions for the year. Their daughter, Gloria, is a sophomore in college. This couple could shave a considerable amount off their tax bill if they use the $3,400 to help Gloria out with groceries and school—something they were likely to do, anyway, but now can deliberately be put to work for them in their overall financial strategy.

Now, I use Mallory and Ralph only as an example—your circumstances may be different—but I think this nicely illustrates the way planning ahead for taxes can save you money.

Assuming a Lower Tax Rate

Many people anticipate being in a lower tax bracket in retirement. It makes sense: You won't be contributing to retirement funds, you'll be drawing from them. And you won't have all those work expenses—work clothes, transportation, etc.

Yet, do you really plan on changing your lifestyle after retirement? Do you plan to cut down on the number of times you eat out, scale back vacations and skimp on travel?

What I see in my office is that many couples spend more in the first few years, or maybe the first decade, of retirement. Sure, later on, that may taper off, but usually only just in time for their budget to be hit with greater health and long-term care expenses. Do you see where this is going? Many people plan as though their taxable income will be lower in retirement and are surprised when the tax bills come in and look more or less the same as they used to. It's better to plan for the worst and hope for the best, wouldn't you agree?

401(k)/IRA

One sometimes unexpected piece of tax planning in retirement is in your 401(k) or IRA. Most of us have one of these accounts or an equivalent. Throughout our working lives, we pay in, dutifully socking away a portion of our earnings in these tax-deferred accounts. There's the rub: tax-deferred. Not tax-free. Very rarely is anything free of taxation, when you get down to it. Using 401(k)s and IRAs in retirement is no different. The taxes the government deferred when you were in your working years are now coming due, and you will pay taxes on the earned income from those accounts at whatever your current tax rate is.

Just to ensure Uncle Sam gets his due, the government also has a required minimum distribution, or RMD, rule. Beginning at age seventy-two, you are required to withdraw a certain minimum amount every year from your 401(k) or IRA, or you will face a 50 percent tax penalty on any RMD monies you should have withdrawn but didn't, and that's on top of income tax.

Of course, there is also the Roth IRA . You can think of the difference between a Roth IRA and a traditional retirement account as the difference between taxing the seed and taxing the harvest. Because Roths are taxed on the front end, there aren't tax penalties for early withdrawals of the principal, nor are there taxes on the growth after you reach age 59 ½. And, perhaps best of all, there are no RMDs. Of course, you must own a Roth account for a minimum of five years before you are able to take advantage of all of its features.

This is one more area where it pays to be aware of your tax bracket. Some people may find it advantageous to "convert" part or all of their traditional retirement account funds to Roth account funds in a year they are in a lower tax bracket, and pay taxes due on the converted amount in that year. Others may opt to put any excess RMDs from their traditional retirement accounts into other products, like investments or insurance products.

Does that make your head spin? Understandable. That's why it's so important to work with a financial professional and tax planner who can help you not only execute these sorts of tax-efficient strategies but also help you understand what you are doing and why.

Someone once said, the only guarantees in life are death and taxes. Another stated, it's not about how much you make, it's about how much you are allowed to keep. Both of these truisms highlight the need for an efficient, knowledgeable, networked approach.

CHAPTER 5

Market Volatility

Up and down. Roller coaster. Merry-go-round. Bulls and bears. Peak-to-trough. Sound familiar? This is the language we use to talk about the stock market. With volatility and spikes, even our language is jarring, bracing, vivid. Still, many financial strategies tend to revolve around market-based products because there is no other financial class that packs the same potential for growth, pound for pound, as stock-based products.

However, along with the potential for growth is the potential for loss. Many of the people I see in my office come in still feeling a bit burned from the market drama of 2000 to 2010. That was a rough stretch.

So how do we balance these factors? How do we try to satisfy both the need for protection and the need for growth?

For one thing, it is important to recognize the value of diversity. Now, I'm not just talking about the diversity of assets among different kinds of stocks, or even different kinds of stocks and bonds. That's only one kind of diversity, but both stocks and bonds, while different, are still market-based products. Just as an incoming tide raises all boats, most market-based products tend to rise or lower as a whole, so diversity among stocks and bonds won't protect your assets during times when the market as a whole is in decline.

In addition to the sort of "horizontal diversity" you have by purchasing a variety of stocks and bonds from different companies, I encourage having "vertical diversity," or diversity among asset classes. This means having different product types, with varying levels of growth potential, liquidity and protection, all in accordance with your unique situation, goals and needs. This approach won't guarantee you a profit or ensure you won't suffer a loss, but it can help smooth out market volatility and seeks to levelized your returns.

I am often asked, "What percentage of my portfolio should be invested in the market?" Each situation is different and an individual's risk tolerance is unique to them, but for those who aren't in a position to sit and drill down into the nuances of their financial situation, I like the Rule of 100 as a general gauge. Have you ever heard someone use the expression "welcome to the new normal"? The Rule of 100 is about how you should invest your money and takes into consideration the old and new normal.

Take your age and subtract it from 100. Example: If you're sixty-five, the rule of 100 states you should have 65 percent of your assets in guaranteed or secure assets and 35 percent can be exposed to risk. The old approach suggests to use primarily bonds as the safe part of your portfolio, but this is now a matter of some debate. What happens if interest rates go up? Bond prices tend to go down. If the stock market goes down and rising interest rates cause bond price to decrease, your portfolio goes down. But there are a number of low risk financial products you can use for the "secure" part of your portfolio. Keep in mind, the Rule of 100 is only a guideline, and your actual percentages will vary based on a number of factors, including your risk tolerance.

The Color of Money

When you're looking at your overall portfolio diversity, part of the equation is knowing which products fit in what category: what has liquidity, what has protection and what has growth potential.

Before we dive into that, keep in mind that these aren't absolutes. You might think of liquidity, growth and protection as primary colors. While some products will look pretty much yellow, red or blue, others will have a mix of characteristics, making them more green, orange or purple.

Growth

I like to think of the growth category as red. It's powerful, it's somewhat volatile and it's also the category where we have the biggest opportunity for growth and loss. Sometimes products in the growth category have a good deal of liquidity but very little protection from loss. These are our market-based products and strategies, so we're thinking mostly shades of red and orange. This is often a good place to be when you're young but its allure often wanes as you get closer to retirement.

- Stocks
- Equities
- Exchange-traded funds
- Mutual funds
- Corporate bonds
- Real estate investment trusts
- Speculations
- Alternative investments

Liquidity

Yellow is my liquid category color. I typically recommend having at least enough yellow money to cover six months' to a year's worth of expenses in case of emergency. Yellow assets don't need a lot of growth potential; they just need to be readily available when we need them without having to pay steep penalties for accessing funds.

- Cash
- Money market accounts

Protection

The color of protection, to me, is blue. Tranquil, peaceful, sure, even if it lacks a certain amount of flash. This is the direction many people move toward as they're nearing retirement. The red, flashy look of stock market returns and the risk of possible overnight losses is less attractive as we near retirement and look for more consistency and reliability. While this category doesn't often come with a lot of liquidity, the products here are backed by an insurance company, a bank or a government entity.

- Certificates of deposit (FDIC-insured)
- Government-based bonds (backed by the federal government)
- Life insurance (backed by the financial strength of the insurance company)
- Annuities (backed by the financial strength of the insurance company)

Dollar-Cost Averaging

With 401(k)s and other market-based retirement products (IRAs, 403(b)s, etc.), when you are investing for the long term, dollar-cost averaging is a concept that is designed to work in your favor. When the market is trending up, if you are consistently paying in money, month over month, great; your investments are growing, and you are adding to your assets. When the market takes a dip, no problem; your dollars buy more shares at a lower price. At some point, the market will likely rebound, in which case your shares have the potential to fatten up and possibly be more valuable than they were before. This phenomenon is what we call dollar-cost averaging.

However, when you are in retirement, this may work against you. You may even hear of "reverse" dollar-cost averaging. Before, when the market lost ground, you were "bargain-shopping"; your dollars purchased more assets at a reduced price. When you are in retirement, you are no longer the purchaser; you are selling. So in a down market, you have to sell more assets to make the same amount of money as you did in a positive market.

I've had lots of people step into my office saying, "My advisor says the market always bounces back and that I have to just hold on for the long term."

There may be some truth in that; the market regularly go and up and down. But the prospect of potentially higher returns in five years may not be very helpful in retirement if you are relying on the income from those returns, for example, to pay this month's electric bill. Also, dollar-cost averaging offers no assurances of profits or guarantees that you won't lose money in the market. That's why at our firm, we specialize in insurance strategies that help provide a reliable stream of income.

For most retirement plans, there is a need for balance investments and insurance products, and both a managed stock portfolio and insurance-based solutions offer such balance to a portfolio. Insurance products can offer guarantees that a stock portfolio cannot. The key to a successful retirement is income. Where is the monthly check going to come from?

I have seen people go broke "literally" investing in the market alone. So what's the solution? The government and large companies offer pensions as a form of guaranteed income in retirement. Those government pensions are typically funded by annuities. With an individual retirement annuity, you can create a guaranteed stream of income with the right type of benefits tailored to your individual needs.

Is There a "Perfect" Product?

To bring us back around to the discussion of protection, growth and liquidity, the ideal product would be a "10" in all three categories, right? Completely guaranteed, doubling in size every few years, accessible whenever you want. Does such a product exist? Anyone who says yes is either ignorant or malevolent.

Instead of running in circles looking for that perfect product, the silver bullet, the unicorn of financial strategies, it's more important to circle back to the concept of a balanced, asset-diverse retirement portfolio.

This is why your interests may be best served when you work with a team of qualified financial professionals who know what various financial products can do and how to use them in your personal retirement plan.

I ask my clients a very simple question: What is the maximum amount of money you could lose in the market before you would feel uncomfortable? The most common answer is 5 to 10 percent. "I've worked too hard for what I have." Some say, "not one penny" and I repeat zero losses and they emphasize "not a penny." For these clients, I consider guaranteed vehicles. One such option is a fixed indexed annuity, or FIA, which offers principal protection with a level of liquidity. Clients can earn interest tied to the performance of an external market index, while never being invested in the market. The annuity also offers the potential for guaranteed income that lasts as long as you live.

CHAPTER 6
Retirement Income

Retirement. For many of us, it's what we've saved for and dreamed of, pinning our hopes to a magical someday. Is that someday filled with traveling? Spoiling the grandkids? Gardening? Maybe your fondest dream is just never having to work again, never having to clock in or be accountable to someone else.

Your ability to do these things all hinges on INCOME. Without the money to support these dreams, even a basic level of work-free lifestyle is often unsustainable. That's why planning for your income in retirement is so crucially foundational. But where to begin?

It can be easy to be overwhelmed by this question. Some may feel the urge to amass a large lump sum and then try to put it all in one product—insurance, investments, liquid assets—to provide all the growth, liquidity and income they need. I think you need a more balanced approach. After all, retirement planning isn't magic. There is no single product that can be all things to all people, or even all things to one person, and no approach works unilaterally for everyone. That's why it's important to talk to a financial professional who can help you lay down the basics and take you step by step through the process. Not only can you have greater assurance that you have addressed the areas you need to, but you will also have an ally who can help you break it down and help keep you from feeling overwhelmed.

Sources of Income

Thinking of all the pieces of your retirement expenses might be intimidating. But, like cleaning out a junk drawer or revisiting that garage remodel, once you have laid everything out, you can begin to push things into categories.

Once you have a good overall picture of where your expenses will lie, you can start stacking up the resources to cover them.

Social Security

Social Security is a guaranteed, inflation-protected federal insurance program that plays a big part in most of our retirement plans. From delaying until you've reached full retirement age or beyond to examining spousal benefits, as I discuss elsewhere in this book, there is plenty you can do to try to make the most of this monthly benefit. As with all of your retirement income sources, it's important to see how to make this resource stretch to give you the most bang and buck for your situation.

Pension

Another generally reliable source of retirement income for you might be a pension, if you are one of the lucky people who still has one.

If you don't have a pension, go ahead and skim on down to the next point, but if you do have a pension, let's take a second.

Because your pension can be such a central piece of your retirement income plan, you will want to put some thought into answering basic questions about it.

How well is your pension funded? Since the heyday of the pension plan, companies and governments have neglected to fund their pension obligations, causing a persistent problem with this otherwise reliable asset. A report by the American Legislative Exchange Council revealed a $5.96 trillion deficit in state pension funds overall in 2018.[10] If you have a pension, it is quite possibly included in that statistic.

In addition to checking up on your pension's health, check into what your options are for withdrawing your pension. If you have already retired and made those decisions, this may be a foregone conclusion. If not, it pays to know what you can expect and what decisions you can make, such as taking spousal options to cover your husband or wife if he or she outlives you.

Also, some companies are incentivizing lump-sum payouts of pensions to reduce the companies' payment liabilities. If that's the case with your employer, talk to your financial professional to see if it might be prudent to do something like that or if it might be better to stick with lifetime payments or other options.

Your 401(k) and IRA

One "modern way" to save for retirement is in a 401(k) or IRA (or their nonprofit or governmental equivalents). These tax-advantaged accounts are, in my opinion, a poor substitute for pensions, but one of the biggest disservices we do to ourselves is to not take full advantage of them in the first place. According to one article, about 42 percent of adults under thirty and 26 percent of adults thirty to forty-four haven't contributed to any retirement account, let alone their 401(k). [11]

Also, if you have changed jobs over the years, do the work of tracking down any benefits from your past employers. You might have an IRA here or a 401(k) there; keep track of

---

[10] Jonathan Williams, Christine Smith, Thurston Powers, and Bob Williams. ALEC. March 20, 2019. "Unaccountable and Unaffordable 2018." https://www.alec.org/publication/unaccountable-and-unaffordable-2018/

[11] Niall McCarthy. Forbes. June 3, 2019. "Report: A Quarter of Americans Have No Retirement Savings." https://www.forbes.com/sites/niallmccarthy/2019/06/03/report-a-quarter-of-americans-have-no-retirement-savings-infographic/#5fb35b703ebf

those so you can pull them together and look at those assets when you're ready to look at establishing sources of retirement income.

Other Assets

- Do you have life insurance?
- Do you have any annuities?
- How about long-term care insurance?
- Any passive income sources?
- Stock and bond portfolios?
- Liquid assets? What's in your bank account?
- Any alternative investments?
- Rental properties?

It's important, if you are going through the work of sitting with a financial professional, to look at your retirement income picture and pull together ALL of your assets, no matter how big or small. From the free insurance policy offered at your bank to the sizable investment in your brother-in-law's modestly successful furniture store, you want to have a good idea of where your money is.

Many couples who visit with me have 401(k)s, IRAs, brokerage accounts, CDs, savings, and checking accounts. They know they have money; they just don't know if it's enough to last their lifetime. They don't understand how and when to access their investments nor do they understand the internal costs and fees associated with their investments. When you have five or six 401(k)s from various employers, bringing them all together in one location simplifies things, making it easier to see how your money can start working for you. This information provides a tremendous personal relief factor.

Retirement Income Needs

How much income will you need in retirement? How do you determine that? A lot of people work toward a random number, thinking, "If I can just have a million dollars, I'll be comfortable in retirement!" Don't get me wrong; it is possible to save up a lot of money and then retire in the hopes that you can keep your monthly expenses lower than some set estimation. But I think this carries a risk of running out of money. Instead, I work with my clients to find out what their current and projected income needs are and then work from there to see how we might cover any gaps between what they have and what they want.

Goals and Dreams

I like to start with your pie in the sky. Do you find yourself planning for your vacations more thoroughly than you do your retirement? A recent survey found one in five Americans spend more time planning our vacations than we spend planning our retirements.[12] Maybe it's because planning a vacation is less stressful: Having a week at the beach go awry is, well, a walk on the beach compared to running out of money in retirement. Whatever the case, perhaps it would be better if you thought of your retirement as a vacation in and of itself—no clocking in, no boss, no overtime. If you felt unlimited by financial strain, what would you do?

Would an endless vacation for you mean Paris and Rome? Would it mean mentoring at children's clubs or serving at the local soup kitchen? Or maybe it would mean deepening your ties to those immediately around you—neighbors, friends and family. Maybe it would mean more time to do hobbies and activities you love. Have you been considering a second (or even

---

[12] Malika Mitra. CNBC. August 2, 2019. "You're not alone if you spend more time planning your vactation than working on your finances." https://www.cnbc.com/2019/08/02/1-in-5-people-spend-more-time-planning-vacations-than-finances-survey.html

third) act as a small business owner, turning a hobby or passion into a revenue source?

This is your time to daydream and answer the question: If you could do anything, what would you do?

After that, it's a matter of putting a dollar amount on it. What are the costs of round-the-world travel? One couple I know said their biggest priority in retirement was being able to take each of their grandchildren on a cross-country vacation every year. That's a pretty specific goal—and one that is reasonably easy to nail down a budget for.

All of us have goals and dreams. If you really look at what people want in life as they get older, it is often the ability to be relevant in the lives of others. When you and loved ones look back, it won't be about how much you made, it will be about the impact you had on the lives of others.

Current Budget

A current expense report is one of the trickiest pieces of retirement spending. Most people assume the expenses of their lives in retirement will be different, lower. After all, there will be no drive to work, no need to keep a formal wardrobe and, perhaps most impactful of all, no more saving for retirement!

Yet, we often underestimate our daily spending habits. That's why I typically ask my clients to bring in their bank statements for the past year—they are reflective of your ACTUAL spending, not just what you think you're spending.

The best way to analyze income needs in retirement is to look at your expenses. Expenses are a road map to show you where you can go. Look at your checkbook over the past six months and take an honest look at how much you are really spending. This is the starting point. Once we determine how much a person is currently spending to facilitate their lifestyle, we talk about things like inflation, retirement goals, bucket-list items, and potential health care needs. After coming up with a number, I work on helping them find the money within their portfolio to accomplish retirement goals and make adjustments, if necessary.

I can't count the number of times I have sat with a couple, asked them about their spending and had them give me a number that seems incredibly low. When I ask them about where it came from, they usually estimated based on their total bills. Yet, our spending is so much more than our mortgage, utilities, cable, phone, car, grocery or credit card bills.

"What about clothes?" I ask, "Or dining out? What about gifts and coffees and last-minute birthday cards?" That's when the lights come on.

This is why I suggest collecting a year's worth of information. There is usually no such thing as a one-time purchase. Did you buy new furniture? Even if that is a rarity, do you think that will be the last time you EVER buy furniture?

I recently got a call from a clients' family member who wanted me to analyze her money. "My account has been going nowhere for the past few years and I have no money." The first thing I did was ask the client about household expenses. Expenses were at $5,000 monthly, or $60,000 yearly. Her net income after taxes was just shy of $100,000. Theoretically she had more than $3,000 a month more than she needed. So, the question became, where is it going? I told her I couldn't help her until she sat down with her spouse and they figured out where the excess funds were going. Some people are in denial about what they are spending. There has to be an awakening or a realization of their financial situation to help them achieve their financial goals.

Another hefty one is spending on the kids. Many of the couples I work with are quick to help their adult children, whether it's something like letting them live in the basement, paying for college, babysitting, paying an occasional bill, or contributing to a grandchild's college fund. They aren't alone— 79 percent of Americans in 2018 said they had provided financial support for an adult child. And it's not unlikely for some parents to tap into their retirement funds to do so.[13]

My clients sometimes protest that what they do for their grown children can stop in retirement. They don't NEED to help. But I get it. Parents like to feel needed. And, while you never want to neglect saving for retirement in favor of taking on financial risks like your child's student debt, the parents who help their adult children do so in part because it helps them feel fulfilled.

When it comes down to expenses, including and especially spending on your family, don't make your initial calculations based on what you COULD whittle your budget down to if you HAD to. Instead, start from where you are. Who wants to live off a bare-bones bank account in retirement?

Other Expenses

Once you have nailed down your current budget and your dreams or goals for retirement, there are a few other outstanding pieces to think about—some expenses that some people don't take the time to consider before making and executing a plan. But I assume you want to get it right, so let's take a look.

Housing

Do you know where you want to live in retirement? This makes up a substantial piece of your income puzzle—since the typical American household owns a home, and it's generally their

---

[13] Lorie Konish. CNBC. October 2, 2018. "Parents Spend Twice as Much on Adult Children than They Save for Retirement."
https://www.cnbc.com/2018/10/02/parents-spend-twice-as-much-on-adult-children-than-saving-for-retirement.html

largest asset—but it often goes unaccounted for until the last minute. [14]

Some people prefer to live right where they are for as long as they can. Others have been waiting for retirement to pull the trigger on an ambitious move. Whatever your plans and whatever your reasons, there are quite a few things to consider.

Mortgage

Do you still have a mortgage? What may have been a nice tax boon in your working years could turn into a financial burden in your retirement. After all, when you are on a limited income, a mortgage is just one more bill sapping your financial strength. It is something to put some thought into, whether you plan to age in place or are considering moving to your dream home, buying a house out of state or living in a retirement community.

Upkeep and Taxes

A house without a mortgage still requires annual taxes. While it's tempting to think of this as a once-a-year expense, when you have limited earning potential, your annual tax bill might be something into which you put a little more forethought.

The costs of homeownership aren't just monetary. When you find yourself dealing with more house than you need, it can drain your time and energy. From keeping clutter at bay to keeping the lawn mower running, upkeep can be extensive and expensive. For some, that's a challenge they heartily accept and can comfortably take on. For others, the idea of yard work or cleaning an area larger than they need feels foolish.

For instance, Peggy discovered after her knee replacement that most of her house was inaccessible to her when she was laid up.

---

[14] Jann Swanson. Mortgage News Daily. August 28, 2019. "Homeownership is the Top Contributor to Household Wealth." http://www.mortgagenewsdaily.com/08282019_homeownership.asp

"It felt ridiculous to pay someone else to dust and vacuum a house I was only living in 40 percent of!"

Practicality and Adaptability

Erik and Magda are looking to retire within the next two decades. They just sold their old three-bedroom ranch-style house. Their twins are in high school, and the couple had wanted to "upgrade" for years. Now they live in a gorgeous 1940s three-story house with all the kitchen space they ever wanted, five sprawling bedrooms and a library and media room for themselves and their children. Within months of moving in, the couple realized that a house perfect for their active teens would no longer be perfect in five to fifteen years.

"We are already paying the mortgage for this house, but we've started saving for the next one," said Magda, "Because who wants to be going up two flights of stairs to their bedroom when they're seventy-eight?"

Others I know have encountered similar situations in their personal lives. After a health crisis, one couple found the luxurious tub for two they slaved over installing had become a specter of a bad slip and safety risks. It's important to think through what your physical reality could be, whatever your long-term plan might be, and I think it's amazing how many people don't.

Contracts and Regulations

If you are looking into a cross-country move, be aware of new tax tables or local ordinances in the area you are looking to move. After all, you don't want to experience sticker-shock when you are looking at downsizing or reducing your bills in retirement.

Along the same lines, if you are moving into a retirement community, be sure to look at the fine print. What will happen if you must move into a different situation for long-term care? Will you be penalized? Will you be responsible for replacing your slot in the community? What are all of the fees, and what do they cover?

Inflation

As I write this in 2020, America has experienced a long stretch of low inflation, with inflation not exceeding 4 percent since 1991.[15]

However, inflation isn't a one-time bump; it has a cumulative effect. Even with relatively low inflation over the past few decades, the $20 sneakers you bought your grade-schooler in 1991 will cost $34.02 to buy for your grandchild in 2020.[16] What if, in retirement, we hit a stretch like the late seventies and early eighties, when annual inflation rates of 10 percent became the norm? It may be wise to consider some extra padding in your retirement income plan to account for any potential increase in inflation in the future.

Aging

Also in the expense category, think about longevity. We all hope to age gracefully. However, it's important to face the prospect of aging with a sense of realism.

The elephant in the room for many families is long-term care: No one wants to admit they will likely need it, but the reality is that it's estimated that as many as 70 percent of us will.[17] Aging is a significant piece of retirement income planning because you'll want to figure out how to set aside money for your care, either at home or away from it. The more comfortable you get with discussing your wishes and plans with

---

[15] US Inflation Calculator. January 2020. "Historical Inflation Rates." http://www.usinflationcalculator.com/inflation/historical-inflation-rates/
[16] Ibid.
[17] LongTermCare.gov. 2020. "The Basics." http://longtermcare.gov/the-basics/

your loved ones, the easier planning for the financial side of it can be.

I discuss health care and potential long-term care costs in more detail elsewhere in this book but suffice it to say that nursing home care can be expensive and typically isn't something you get plan out ahead of time and decide when in the future you will need it.

It isn't just the costs of long-term care that pose a concern in living longer. It's also about covering the possible costs of everything else associated with living longer. For instance, if Henry retires from his job as a biochemical engineer at age sixty-five, perhaps he planned to have a very decent income for twenty years, until age eighty-five. But what if he lives until he's ninety-fivee? That's a whole third more—ten years—of personal income he will need.

Putting It All Together

Whew! So, you have pulled together what you have, and you have a pretty good idea of where you want to be. Now your financial professional and you can go about the work of arranging what you have to help cover what you need—and how you might try to cover any gaps you have.

Like the proverbial man in the Bible who built his house on a rock, I like to help my clients figure out how to cover their day-to-day living expenses—their needs—with insurance and other guaranteed income sources like pensions and Social Security.

Can you retire? The first step in determining this is to look at your anticipated monthly expenses. The second step is to look at all your possible income sources, your Social Security income, pensions, annuities, *all* of your income sources. If you have three or four 401(k)s and IRAs with former employers, we might want to simplify things and put them in one location. Once we have gathered up all of your assets, we can determine if—and more importantly, when—you can retire. If someone can retire and chooses not to, that's obviously a good position to be in. I've had clients tell me that when they realize that they work because they want to, not because they have to, their attitude and therefore lives are changed for the better.

Again, you should keep in mind that there isn't one single financial vehicle, asset or source that can fill all of your needs, and that's OK. One of the challenges of making a plan for your income in retirement is about figuring out what products to use. You can let go of some of that stress when you accept that you will need a diverse portfolio, not just one massive money pile.

One way to help shore up your income gaps is by working with your financial professional and a qualified tax advisor to mitigate your tax exposure. Effective tax planning isn't about "adding" to your income; especially with retirement, it's less about what you make as it is about what you keep. Paying a lower tax bill keeps more money in your pocket, which is where you want it when it comes to retirement income.

Now you can look at ways to cover your remaining retirement goals. Are there products like long-term-care insurance that are specific to a certain kind of expense you anticipate? Is there a particular asset you want to use for your "play" money—that money for trips and gifting for the grandkids? Is there any way you can portion off money for those charitable legacy plans?

Once you have analyzed your income wants and needs and your realistic assets to cover them, you may have a gap. The masterstroke of a competent financial professional will be to help you figure out how you will cover that gap. Will you perhaps need to cut out a round of golf a week? Maybe skip the new car? Or will you need to take more significant action?

One way to cover an income gap is to consider working longer before retirement or part time even after that magical calendar date. This may not be the best "plan" for you; disabilities, work demands and physical or emotional limitations can stymie the best-laid plans to continue working.

However, if it is physically possible for you, this is one big way to help your assets last, for more than one reason.

In fact, about one in five Americans are still working past age sixty-five. This is a record percentage in the past half-century. While some do list their personal finances as a reason for staying on the job, others do so to avoid feeling bored in retirement, among other reasons.[18]

I will share a story about a couple we will call Don and Jane. Don was sixty-four years old and his wife, Jane was sixty-two. Because they were referred by trusted friends, they had a lot of confidence in me before we met. I asked them what their ultimate goal was, and Don said, "I want my wife to walk into her job and quit on Friday." Our meeting was on a Wednesday. After an hour and a half, I had enough information and I said, "I think I can help accomplish your goal," and we set up an appointment for the following week. Keep in mind, I didn't think Don was serious when he told me he wanted his wife to quit her job—I often have people say things like this to me when it is clearly impractical or hyperbolic.

The following week, we all sat down and reviewed their retirement plan. They were extremely excited, and informed me that, after the first meeting, Jane had in fact gone that Friday and quit her job. Now, what they had discovered in our previous meeting was that they had saved quite a bit beyond what they originally thought, and even before we put a plan in place, they were confident in the amount they had saved. Yet, while I was relieved that it looked like it would work for them, it is a good idea to have a plan in place *before* quitting your job. Planning ahead is, in my experience, usually more freeing than making a plan that *has* to work on the fly. As they say, "nothing like a little pressure."

---

[18] Associated Press. October 9, 2018. "1 in 5 Americans over 65 are Still Waiting to Retire." https://nypost.com/2018/10/09/1-in-5-americans-over-65-are-still-waiting-to-retire/.

When you're retired, you no longer have an employer paying you a steady check. It is up to you to make sure you have saved and planned for the income you need.

CHAPTER 7

Longevity

You would think the prospect of the grave would loom more frightening as we age, yet many retirees list the fear of running out of money in their twilight years as their No. 1 biggest fear.[19] This fear is, unfortunately, justified, in part because of one big factor: We're living longer.

According to the U.S. Census, in 1950, the average life expectancy for a sixty-five-year-old male was seventy-eight, and the average for females was eighty-one. In 2010, it was closer to eighty-four and eighty-six, respectively.[20]

The bottom line of many retirees' budget woes comes down to this: They just didn't plan to live as long. Now, when we are young and in our working years, that's not something we necessarily see as a bad thing; don't some people fantasize about living forever, or at least reaching the ripe old age of 100?

However, with a longer lifespan, as we near retirement, we face a few snags. Our resources are finite—we only have so much money to provide income—but our lifespans can be unpredictably long, perhaps longer than our resources allow. Also, longer lives don't necessarily equate with healthier lives.

---

[19] Samiha Khanna. Journal of Accountancy. February 14, 2019. "Clients' Top Fear: Running out of Money."
https://www.journalofaccountancy.com/news/2019/feb/top-retirement-fears-201920387.html
[20] Social Security Administration. 2011 Trustees Report. "Actuarial Publications: Cohort Life Expectancy."
https://www.ssa.gov/oact/tr/2011/lr5a4.html.

The longer you live, the more money you will likely need to spend on health care, even excluding long-term care needs like nursing homes.

You will also run into inflation. If you don't plan to live another twenty-five years but end up doing so, inflation at an average 2.5 percent will raise your $50,000-per-year budgeted need up to $93,000 per year. Or, if you live another eight years as inflation rises, you will need about $810,000 to cover those same expenses.[21] And this is before you count the expenses of any potential healthcare or long-term care needs.

Because we don't necessarily get to have our cake and eat it, too, our collective increased longevity hasn't necessarily increased the healthy years of our lives. Typically, our life-extending care most widely applies to the time in our lives where we will need more care in general. Think of common situations like a pacemaker at eighty-five, or cancer treatment at seventy-eight.

"Wow, Ron," I can hear you say, "way to start with the good news first."

I know, I've painted a grim picture. But all I'm concerned about here is the cost. It's hard to put a dollar sign on life, but that is essentially what we're talking about when discussing longevity and your finances. According to the Stanford Center on Longevity, more than half of pre-retirees underestimate the life expectancy of the average sixty-five-year-old.[22] Living longer isn't a bad thing; it just costs more, and one key to a sound retirement strategy is preparing in advance for that expense.

One woman I know of illustrates this picture perfectly. Her mother passed away in her late seventies after years of suffering

---

[21] Katie Brockman. The Motley Fool. August 19, 2018. "More Americans are Living into Their 90s—and That's Bad News for Their Savings." https://www.fool.com/retirement/2018/08/19/more-americans-are-living-into-their-90s-and-thats.aspx

[22] Stanford Center on Longevity. "Underestimating Years in Retirement." http://longevity.stanford.edu/underestimating-years-in-retirement/

from Alzheimer's disease. Her father died at eighty from cancer. With modern medicine and treatment, this woman survived two rounds of breast cancer, lived with diabetes, and endured a pacemaker, extending her life to age eighty-eight, nearly a decade beyond what she anticipated. However, she and her husband had saved and planned for "just in case," trying to be prepared just in case they had to move, just in case they needed nursing home care, just in case they needed to help children and grandchildren with their expenses. One of their just-in-case scenarios was just in case they lived much longer than they anticipated. The last six years of her life were fraught with medical expenses, but she was also blessed with knowing her five great-grandchildren and deepening relationships with her children and grandchildren. She was able to pay for her own medical care, including her final two years in a nursing home, and her twilight years were truly golden. From age eighty-five to eighty-eight, she was more socially active, with many visits from family and friends, and she participated in more activities than she had in the seven years since her husband died. When she, too, passed away, her planning from decades earlier allowed her to pass on a legacy to her children, in some ways that can be calculated in dollar signs *and* in ways that can't.

Living longer may be more expensive, but it can be so meaningful when you plan for what-ifs and just-in-cases.

Retiring Later

Planning for a long life in retirement partly comes down to when you retire. While many people end up retiring earlier than they anticipated due to injuries, layoffs, family crises and other unforeseen circumstances, continuing to work past age sixty and even sixty-five is still a viable option for others and can be an excellent way to help establish financial comfort in retirement.

There are many reasons for this. For one, you obviously still earn a paycheck and the benefits that go with it. Medical coverage and beefing up your retirement accounts with further savings can be pretty significant by themselves, but the advantage of continuing your income is also that it should keep you from dipping into your retirement funds, further allowing them the opportunity to grow.

Additionally, for many workers, their 8-to-5 is more than just clocking in and out. Having a sense of purpose can keep us active physically, mentally and socially. That kind of activity and level of engagement may also help stave off many of the health problems that plague retirees. Avoiding a sedentary life is one of the advantages of staying plugged into the workforce, if possible.

Working because you want to is different than working because you have to. I have clients who continue to work well into their sixties and early seventies, because they still have something to offer. They also knew, when they are ready to leave the workforce, their income will continue because of the plan they have in place.

Health Care

Take a second to reflect on your health care plan. Although working up to or even past age sixty-five would allow you to avoid a coverage gap between your working years and Medicare, that may not be an option for you. Even if it is, when you retire, you will need to make some decisions about what kind of insurance coverage you may need to supplement your Medicare. Are there any medical needs you have that may require coverage in addition to Medicare? Did your parents or grandparents have any inherited medical conditions you might consider using a special savings plan to cover?

These are all questions that are important to review with your financial professional so you can be sure you have enough money put aside for health care.

Long-Term Care

Longevity means the need for long-term care is more statistically likely. If you intend to pass on a legacy, planning for long-term care is paramount, since it's estimated that as many as three-fourths of us will need it,[23] yet this may be one of the biggest, most stressful pieces of longevity planning that I encounter in my work. For one thing, who wants to talk about the point in their lives when they may feel the most limited? Who wants to dwell on what will happen if they no longer can toilet, bathe, dress or feed themselves?

I get it; this is a less-than-fun part of planning. But a little bit of preparation now can go a long way!

When it comes to your longevity, just like with your goals, one of the important things to do is sit and dream. It may not be the fun, road-trip-to-the-Grand-Canyon kind of dreaming, but spend time envisioning how you want your twilight years to look.

For instance, if it is important for you to live in your home for as long as possible, who will provide for the day-to-day fixes and to-dos of housework if you become ill? Will you set aside money for a service, or do you have relatives or friends near at hand whom you would comfortably allow to help you? Do you have a preference for in-home care over nursing homes or assisted living? This could be a good time to discuss the possibility of moving into a retirement community versus staying where you are, or whether it's worth moving to another state and leaving relatives behind.

These are all important factors to discuss with your spouse and children, as *now* is the best time to address questions and concerns. For instance, is aging in place more important to one spouse than the other? Are the friends or relatives who live

---

[23] LongTermCare.gov. 2020. "How Much Care Will You Need?" https://longtermcare.acl.gov/the-basics/how-much-care-will-you-need.html.

nearby emotionally, physically and financially capable of helping you for a time if you have an illness?

Many families I meet with find these conversations very uncomfortable, particularly when children discuss nursing home care with their parents. A knee-jerk reaction for many is to promise that they will care for their aging parents. This is noble and well-intentioned, but there needs to be an element of realism here. Does "help" from an adult child mean they stop by and help you with laundry, cooking, home maintenance and bills? Or does it mean they move you into their spare room when you have hip surgery? Are they prepared to help you toilet and bathe if that becomes difficult for you to do on your own?

I don't mean to discourage families from caring for their own; this can be a profoundly admirable relationship when it works out. However, I've seen families put off planning for late-in-life care based on a tenuous promise that the adult children would care for their parents, only to watch as the support system crumbles. Sometimes this is because the assumed caregiver hasn't given serious thought to the preparation they would need, both in a formal sense and with regard to their personal physical, emotional and financial commitments. This is often also because we can't see the future: Alzheimer's and other maladies of old age can exact a heavy toll. When a loved one gets to the point that he or she is at risk of wandering away or needs help with two or more activities of daily living, it can be more than one person, or one family can realistically handle.

If you know what you want, communicate with your family about both the best-case and worst-case scenarios. Then, hope for the best and plan for the worst.

Realistic Cost of Care

Wrapped up in your planning should be a consideration for the cost of long-term care. Although many of us will need some degree of long-term care—including the 30 percent of us who may need up to five years of facility care—60 percent of us underestimate the costs of nursing home care. On average, consumers underestimate the annual cost of a private room in a nursing home by 51 percent.[24]

Another piece of planning for long-term care costs is anticipating inflation. It's common knowledge prices have been and keep rising, and that will lower your purchasing power on everything from food to medical care. Long-term care is a big piece of the inflation-disparity pie, which is part of why many find their estimates of nursing home care widely miss the mark. According to one survey, people expected to pay around $25,350 in out-of-pocket long-term care expenses per year, but, in reality, they'll more likely be paying over $47,000.[25]

While local costs vary from state to state, here's the national median for various forms of long-term care (plus projections that account for a 3 percent annual inflation, so you can see what I'm talking about):[26]

---

[24] Tamara E. Holmes. Yahoo Finance. July 24, 2019. "Consumers Underestimate Costs of Long-Term Care." https://finance.yahoo.com/news/consumers-underestimate-costs-long-term-173542918.html
[25] Moll Law Group. 2019. "The Cost of Long-Term Care." https://www.molllawgroup.com/the-cost-of-long-term-care.html
[26] Genworth Financial. June 2018. "Cost of Care Survey 2018." https://www.genworth.com/aging-and-you/finances/cost-of-care.html

Long-Term Care Costs: Inflation				
	Home Health Care, Homemaker Services	Adult Day Care	Assisted Living	Nursing Home (semi-private room)
Annual 2019	$51,480	$19,500	$48,612	$90,155
Annual 2029	$69,185	$26,206	$65,330	$121,161
Annual 2039	$92,979	$35,219	$87,799	$162,830
Annual 2049	$124,955	$47,332	$117,994	$218,830

Fund Your Long-Term Care

One big "doing it wrong" that I see are those who haven't planned for long-term care because they assume the government will take care of everything. But that's a huge misconception. The government has two health insurance programs: Medicare and Medicaid. These can greatly assist you in your health care needs in retirement but usually don't provide enough coverage to cover all of your health care costs in retirement. My firm isn't a government outpost, so we don't get to make decisions when it comes to forming policy and specifics about either one of these programs. I'm going to give the overview of both, but if you want to get into the details of these programs, you can visit Medicare.gov and Medicaid.gov.

Medicare
Medicare covers those age sixty-five and older and the disabled. Medicare's coverage of any nursing-home-related health issues

is limited. It might cover your nursing home stay if it is not a "custodial" stay and it isn't long term. For example, if you break a bone or suffer a stroke and stay in a nursing home for rehabilitative care and then return home, Medicare may cover you. But if you have developed dementia or are looking to move to a nursing facility because you can no longer bathe, dress, toilet, feed yourself, take care of your hygiene, etc., then Medicare is not going to pay for your nursing home costs.[27]

Medicaid
Medicaid is a program that the states administer, so funding, protocol and limitations vary. Compared to Medicare, Medicaid more widely covers nursing home care, but it targets a different demographic than Medicare: those with low incomes.

If you have more assets than the Medicaid limit in your state and need nursing home care, you will need to use those assets to pay for your care. You will also have a list of additional state-approved ways to spend some of these assets over the Medicaid limit, such as pre-purchasing burial plots and funeral expenses, or paying off debts. After that, your remaining assets fund your nursing home stay until they are gone, at which point Medicaid will jump in.

Some people aren't stymied by this, thinking they will just pass on their financial assets early, gifting them to relatives, friends and causes so they can qualify for Medicaid when they need it. However, to prevent this exact scenario, Uncle Sam has implemented the look-back period. Currently, if you enroll in Medicaid, you are subject to having the government scrutinize the last five years of your finances for large gifts or expenses that may subject you to penalties, temporarily making you ineligible for Medicaid coverage.

So, if you're planning to preserve your money for future generations and retain control of your financial resources

---

[27] Medicare.gov. "What Part A covers." https://www.medicare.gov/what-medicare-covers/part-a/what-part-a-covers.html

during your life, you'll probably want to prepare for the costs of longevity beyond a "government plan."

Self-Funding

One way to fund a longer life is the old-fashioned way, through self-funding. There are a variety of financial tools you can use, and they all have their pros and cons. If your assets are in low-interest accounts (savings, bonds, CDs), you risk letting inflation erode the value of your dollar. Or, if you are relying on the stock market, you have more growth potential, but you'll also want to consider the possible implications of market volatility; what if your assets take a hit? If you suffer a loss in your retirement portfolio in early or mid-retirement, you might have the option to "tighten your belt," so to speak, and cut back on discretionary spending to allow your portfolio the room to bounce back. But if you are retired and depend on income from a stock account that just hit a downward stride, what are you going to do?

HSAs

These days, you might also be able to self-fund through a health savings account, or HSA, if you have access to one through a high-deductible health plan (you will not qualify to save in an HSA after enrolling in Medicare). In an HSA, any growth of your tax-deductible contributions will be tax-free, and any distributions that are paid out for qualified health costs are also tax-free. That can be a tax trifecta. Long-term care expenses count as health costs, so, if this is an option available to you, that is one way to use the tax advantages to self-fund your longevity. Bear in mind, if you are younger than sixty-five, any money you use for nonqualified expenses will be subject to taxes and penalties, and, if you are older than sixty-five, any HSA money you use for non-medical expenses is subject to income tax.

LTCI

One slightly more nuanced way to pay for longevity, specifically for long-term care, is long-term-care insurance, or LTCI. As car insurance protects your assets in case of a car accident, and home insurance protects your assets in case something happens to your house, long-term care insurance aims to protect your assets in case you need long-term care in an at-home or nursing home situation.

As with other types of insurance, you will pay a monthly premium in exchange for an insurance company to pay for long-term care down the road. Typically, policies cover two to three years of care, which is adequate for an "average" situation: it's estimated that up to 70 percent of Americans will need about three years of long-term care of some kind. However, it's important to consider that you might not be "average" when you are preparing for long-term care costs; one third of today's sixty-five-year-olds could need care for longer than five years.[28]

Now, there are a few oft-cited components of LTCI that make it unattractive for some:

- Expense—LTCI is expensive. It is generally less expensive the younger you are, but a fifty-five-year-old couple who purchased LTCI in 2019 could expect to pay $3,050 each year for an average three-year coverage policy. And the annual cost only increases from there the older you are.[29]
- Limited options—Let's face it: LTCI is expensive for some consumers, but it is also expensive for companies

---

[28] LongTermCare.gov. 2020. "How Much Care Will You Need?" https://longtermcare.acl.gov/the-basics/how-much-care-will-you-need.html.
[29] American Association for Long-Term Care Insurance. January 2019. "2019 National Long-Term Care Insurance Price Index." https://www.aaltci.org/news/wp-content/uploads/2019/01/2019-Price-Index-LTC.pdf

that offer it. With fewer companies willing to take on that expense, that narrows the market, meaning opportunities to price shop for plans with different options or custom plans are limited.

- If you know you need it, you may not be able to get it—Insurance companies that offer LTCI are taking on a risk that you may need LTCI. That risk is the foundation of the product—you may or may not need it. If you know you will need it because you have a dementia diagnosis or another illness for which you will need long-term care, you will likely not qualify for LTCI coverage.
- Use it or lose it—If you have LTCI and are in the minority of Americans who die having never needed long-term care, all the money you paid into your LTCI plan is gone.
- Possibly fluctuating premium rates—Your rate is not locked in on LTCI. Companies maintain the ability to raise or lower your premium amounts. This means some seniors face an ultimatum: Keep funding a policy at what might be a less affordable rate OR lose coverage and let go of all the money they paid in thus far.

After that, you might be thinking, "How can people possibly be interested in LTCI?" But let me repeat myself—as many as 70 percent of Americans will need long-term care. And, although only 8 percent of Americans have purchased LTCI, keep in mind the high cost of nursing home care. Can you afford $7,000 a month to put into nursing home care and still have enough left over to protect your legacy? This is a very real concern: One study says 72 percent of Americans are impoverished by the end of just one year in a nursing home.[30] So, not to sound like a broken record, but it is vitally important

---

[30] A Place for Mom. January 2018. "Long-Term Care Insurance: Costs & Benefits." http://www.aplaceformom.com/senior-care-resources/articles/long-term-care-costs.

to have a plan in place to deal with longevity and long-term care if you intend to leave a financial legacy.

Long-Term and Home Health Care

The Problem:

I started in the business back in 1985. I represented all three companies available at that time for this marketplace. None of these companies provided home health care insurance. The insurance at the time was designed to provide coverage in the areas Medicare did not. Medicare provided benefits for skilled nursing care only. A very small percentage of people back then and even today, ever spend time in skilled nursing care. The majority of the time was spent in intermediate or custodial care. This is why the insurance industry created coverage for those levels of care. They offered what we call use-it-or-lose-it policies. If you didn't use the coverage you lost all the monies that you paid into the company.

The challenge I faced as an agent was most people considered nursing homes as "heaven's gate" or, in other words, it was the last stop before you passed away. Home health care or assisted living facilities weren't common services thirty years ago. Today, this is the most desirable feature of the policies being offered. Individuals who purchased those contracts that offered only intermediate or custodial care were unable to use the coverage for home health care or assisted living facilities because it wasn't written in the contracts at that time. In fact, because no one ever considered that type of coverage would be necessary, it wasn't even offered as an option of care.

If you have long-term or home health care coverage here are some questions you need to ask yourself:
1. If you have coverage purchased many years ago, does it offer you protection for outdated services?

2. If you don't use the benefits, will all those premiums be lost to the insurance company, reimbursed to you, or can you pass those monies on to your beneficiaries?
3. Do you have reimbursement coverage, where you have to submit qualified bills which are reviewed and must be approved in order to receive a payment from the insurance company?

Question 3 is important because you can have a $5,000 a month benefit but receive only $2,500 in reimbursement because the review of your monthly bills only qualifies for that reimbursement amount. With the advancements in medicine and new forms of services that will be offered in the future, most contracts written today will not address future costs because they don't even know what care will look like in twenty to thirty years based on what medical advancements will take place. Remember, these contracts that insurance companies abide by use very specific language, guidelines, and benefits.

Perfection does not exist in any of these contracts, as not every policy will offer every single benefit listed previously. The important thing is to know in advance what your contract will and won't do before an event takes place. Preparation and knowledge are key!

Some Solutions:

I am a firm believer that individuals seeking this type of care are doing so for peace-of-mind purposes. They have had a loved one or close friend who has experienced financial hardship due to lack of coverage. A long-term care stay can cause financial ruin to a person's financial situation if they don't properly prepare. I have used a number of strategies over the years to help clients accomplish their goals. Below you will see a couple of options and strategies that I've used in the past. Just because this was the right strategy for them doesn't mean it's the right strategy for you, of course, but I'd like you to understand there are different options for people based on their situations and circumstances.

1. One option is to take an appreciated insurance contract such as an annuity or life insurance contract and perform a 1035 exchange (a sort of transfer of money that doesn't change its tax status) into an approved long-term or home health care policy, which could eliminate any tax consequences. Many individuals have insurance contracts that have gains, but they do not want to cash in the contracts due to potential tax consequences. According to IRS Code 7702, the following may be an option. Assuming an individual purchased variable annuity with $150,000 as an initial deposit many years ago and the current value was over $300,000. After reviewing the fees they pay, they decide to explore other options. They could cash it in, however, this option could incur close to $40,000 in taxes. Another option is, if they qualify through medical underwriting, they could take the $300,000 and convert it into more than $900,000 in a long-term care policy that offered home health care benefits. If they were to use all the benefits, the monthly payout they would receive, including the $150,000 gain, could be considered a non-taxable event. In the event they both passed away without use any of the benefits, the beneficiaries would receive the original $300,000 deposited to purchase this contract, plus any gains, as a part of their inheritance. The beneficiaries would then be responsible for any gains above the original cost basis at their tax bracket.
2. Individuals may have money sitting in a CD or savings account earning minimal interest. An option with one company is to use the funds to purchase an annuity that offers long-term and home health care benefits. These benefits are often an additional option, available at an added annual cost. If you need coverage for a health care event, the annuity will often pay out two to three times the

normal income payment for a certain number of years to help cover your expenses. And if you end up not needing to use the long-term care or home health care benefits during your lifetime, you pass any remaining annuity benefit to your beneficiaries at your death so you haven't lost all the premiums you paid.

LTCI and self-funding are not the only ways to plan for the expenses of longevity. Some companies are getting creative with their products, particularly insurance companies. One way they are retooling to meet people's needs is through optional product riders on annuities and life insurance. Elsewhere in this book, I talk about annuity basics, and here's a brief overview: Annuities are insurance contracts. You pay the insurance company a premium, either as a lump sum or as a series of payments over a set amount of time, in exchange for guaranteed income payments. One of the advantages of an annuity is that it has access to riders, which allow you to tweak your contract for a fee, usually about 1 percent of the contract value annually. One annuity rider that some companies offer is a long-term-care rider. If you have an annuity with a long-term-care rider and are not in need of long-term care, your contract behaves as any annuity contract would—nothing changes. Generally speaking, if you reach a point when you can't perform multiple functions of daily life on your own, you notify the insurance company, and a representative will turn on those provisions of your contract.

Like LTCI, different companies and products offer different options. Some annuity long-term-care riders offer coverage of two years in a nursing home situation. Others cap expenses at two times the original annuity's value. It greatly depends. Some people prefer this option because there isn't a "use-it-or-lose-it" piece; if you die without ever having needed long-term care, you still will have had the income benefit from the base contract. Still, as with any annuities or insurance contracts, there are the usual restrictions and limitations. Withdrawing money from the contract will affect future income payments, early distributions can result in a penalty, income taxes may apply and, because the insurance company's solvency is what guarantees your payments, it's important to do your research about the insurance company you are considering purchasing a contract from.

Understandably, a discussion on long-term care and its particulars is bound to feel at least a little tedious. Yet, this is a critical piece of planning for income in retirement, particularly if you want to leave a legacy.

Spousal Planning

One thing to keep in mind no matter how you plan to save: Many of us will be planning for more than ourselves. Look back at all the stats on health events and the likelihood of long life and long-term care. If they hold true for a single individual, then the likelihood of having a costly health or long-term care event is even higher for a married couple. And you'll be planning for not just one life but two. So, when it comes to long-term-care insurance, or annuities, or self-funding, or whatever strategy you are looking at utilizing, be sure you are funding longevity for both of you.

CHAPTER 8

Social Security

Social Security is often the foundation piece of retirement income. Backed by the strength of the U.S. Treasury, it provides perhaps the most dependable paycheck you will have in retirement.

From the time you collect your first paycheck from whatever job made you a bonafide taxpayer (for me, it was a busboy at my parent's restaurant in California), you are paying into the grand old Social Security system. What grew and developed out of the pressures of the Great Depression has become one of the most popular government programs in the country, and if you pay in the equivalent of 10 years or more, you, too, can benefit from the Social Security program.

Now, before we get into the nitty-gritty of Social Security, I'd like to address a current concern: Will Social Security still be there for you when you reach retirement age?

The Future of Social Security

This question is ever-present as headlines trumpet an underfunded Social Security program, alongside the flux of baby boomers who are retiring in droves and the comparatively smaller younger generations who are bearing the responsibility of funding the system.

The Social Security Administration itself is a source of this concern as each Social Security statement now bears an asterisk that continues near the end of the summary:

> "*Your estimated benefits are based on current law. Congress has made changes to the law in the past and can do so at any time. The law governing benefit amounts may change because, by 2034, the payroll taxes collected will be enough to pay only about 79 percent of scheduled benefits."

Just a reminder, as if you needed one, that nothing in life is guaranteed.

Before you get too discouraged, though, here are a few thoughts to keep you going:
- Although those who retire after 2034 may only receive 79 cents on the dollar for their scheduled benefits, 79 percent is notably not zero.
- The Social Security Administration has made changes in the distant and near past to protect the fund's solvency, including increasing retirement ages and striking certain filing strategies.
- There are many changes that Congress could make and that lawmakers are currently discussing to fix the system, such as further increasing full retirement age and eligibility.
- One thing that no one is seriously discussing? Reneging on current obligations to retirees or the soon-to-retire.

Take heart. The real answer to the question, "Will Social Security be there for me?" is still yes.

This question is an important one to consider when you take a look at how much we, as a nation, rely on this program. Did you know Social Security benefits compose an average of 33 percent of retired Americans' income? Nearly half of couples and more than 70 percent of unmarried people report their benefits make up more than 50 percent of their income.[31]

If you ask me, that's a pretty significant piece of your retirement income puzzle.

Another caveat? You may not realize this, but no one can legally "advise" you about your Social Security benefits.

"But, Ron," you may be thinking, "Isn't that part of what you do? And what about that nice gentleman at the Social Security Administration office I spoke with on the phone?"

Don't get me wrong. Social Security Administration employees know their stuff. They are trained to know policies and programs, and they are usually pretty quick to tell you what you can and cannot do. But the government specifically says that, because Social Security is a benefit that you alone have paid into and earned, your Social Security decisions, too, are yours alone.

When it comes to financial professionals, we can't push you in any directions, either, BUT—there's a big but, here—working with a well-informed financial professional is still incredibly handy when it comes to your Social Security decisions. Why? Because someone who's worth his or her salt will know what withdrawal strategies might pertain to your specific situation and will ask questions that can help you determine what you are looking for when it comes to your Social Security.

For instance, some people want the highest possible monthly benefit. Others want to start their benefits early—and not always because of financial need. I heard of one man who called in to start his Social Security payments the day he qualified, just because he liked to think of it as the government paying back a debt it owed him and enjoyed the feeling of receiving a check from Uncle Sam.

Whatever your reasons, questions or feelings regarding Social Security, the decision is yours alone, but working with a

---

[31] Social Security Administration. "Fact Sheet: Social Security." https://www.ssa.gov/news/press/factsheets/basicfact-alt.pdf.

financial professional can help you put your options in perspective by showing you—both with industry knowledge and with various software or planning processes—where your benefits fit into your overall strategy for retirement income.

One reason the federal government doesn't allow for "advice" related to Social Security, I suspect, is so no one can profit from giving you advice related to your Social Security benefit—or from providing any clarifications. Again, this is a sign of a good financial professional. Those who are passionate about their work will be knowledgeable about what benefit strategies might be to your advantage and will happily share those possible options with you.

Full Retirement Age

When it comes to Social Security, it seems like many people only think so far as "yes." They don't take the time to understand the various options available. Instead, because it is common knowledge you can begin your benefits at age sixty-two, that's what many of us do. While more people are opting to delay taking benefits, age sixty-two is still firmly the most popular age to start.[32]

What many people fail to understand is that, by starting benefits early, they may be leaving a lot of money on the table. You see, the Social Security Administration bases your monthly benefit on two factors: your earnings history and your full retirement age (FRA).

From your earnings history, they pull the thirty-five years you made the most money and use a mathematical indexing formula to figure out a monthly average from those years. If you paid into the system for less than thirty-five years, then every year you didn't pay in will be counted as a zero.

---

[32] Elizabeth O'Brien. Money. March 7, 2019. "This is the Age when Most People Claim Social Security—and When Experts Say You Really Should." http://money.com/money/5637694/this-is-the-age-when-most-people-claim-social-security-and-when-experts-say-you-really-should/

Once they have calculated what your monthly earning would be at FRA, the government then calculates what to put on your check based on how close you are to FRA. FRA was originally set at sixty-five, but, as the population aged and lifespans lengthened, the government shifted FRA later and later based on an individual's year of birth. Check out the following chart to see when you will reach FRA.

Age to Receive Full Social Security Benefits*	
(Called "full retirement age" or "normal retirement age.")	
Year of Birth*	FRA
1937 or earlier	65
1938	65 and 2 months
1939	65 and 4 months
1940	65 and 6 months
1941	65 and 8 months
1942	65 and 10 months
1943-1954	66
1955	66 and 2 months
1956	66 and 4 months
1957	66 and 6 months
1958	66 and 8 months
1959	66 and 10 months
1960 and later	67

If you were born on Jan. 1 of any year, you should refer to the previous year. (If you were born on the 1st of the month, we figure your benefit (and your full retirement age) as if your birthday was in the previous month.)

When you attain FRA, you are eligible to receive 100 percent of whatever the Social Security Administration says is your full monthly benefit. This is why sixty-six is the second-most popular age to claim: Baby boomers largely reach FRA at sixty-six.[33]

Starting at age sixty-two, for every year before FRA you claim benefits, your monthly check is reduced by 5 percent. Conversely, for every year you delay taking benefits past FRA, your monthly benefit increases by 8 percent (until age seventy—after that, there is no monetary advantage to delaying Social Security benefits). While your circumstances and needs may vary, this is why a lot of financial professionals urge people to at least consider delaying until seventy.

Why Wait?

Taking benefits early could affect your monthly check by _____.								
62	63	64	65	FRA 66	67	68	69	70
-20%	-15%	-10%	-5%	0	+8%	+16%	+24%	+32%

My Social Security

As long as you are over age thirty, you have probably received a notice from the Social Security Administration telling you to activate something called My Social Security. This is a handy way to learn more about whatever your particular benefit options are and to keep track of what your earnings record looks like and the benefits you have accrued over the years.

Essentially, My Social Security is an online account that you can activate to see what your personal Social Security picture looks like, which you can do at www.ssa.gov/myaccount. This can be extremely helpful when it comes to planning for income

---

[33] Ibid.

in retirement and figuring up the difference between your anticipated income versus anticipated expenses.

One other way My Social Security is helpful? It's a great way to see if there is a problem. For instance, I have heard of one woman who, through diligently checking her tax records against her Social Security profile, discovered her Social Security check was shortchanging her, based on her earnings history. After taking the discrepancy to the Social Security Administration, they sent her what they owed her in makeup benefits.

COLA

Social Security is a largely guaranteed piece of the retirement puzzle: If you get a statement that says to expect $1,000 a month, you can pretty surely know you will get $1,000 a month. But there is one detail that is variable, and that is something called the cost-of-living adjustment, or COLA.

The COLA is an increase in your monthly check that is meant to address inflation in everyday life. After all, your expenses will likely continue to experience inflation in retirement, but you will no longer have the opportunity for raises, bonuses or promotions that you had when you were working. Instead, Social Security receives an annual cost-of-living increase tied to the Department of Labor's Consumer Price Index for Urban Wage Earners and Clerical Workers, or CPI-W. If the CPI-W measurement shows inflation rose a certain amount for regular goods and services, then Social Security recipients will see that reflected in their COLA.

The COLA averages 4 percent, but in a no- or low-inflation environment, such as in 2010, 2011 and 2016, Social Security recipients will not get an adjustment. Some see the COLA as a perk, bump or bonus, but in reality it works more like this: Your mom sends you to the store with $2.50 for a gallon of milk. Milk costs exactly $2.50. The next week, you go back with that same amount, but it is now $2.52 for a gallon, so you go back to Mom, and she gives you 2 cents. You aren't bringing home more milk—it just costs more money.

So the COLA is less about "making" more money and more about keeping seniors' purchasing power from eroding when inflation is a big factor, such as in 1975, when it was 8 percent![34] Still, don't let that detract from your enthusiasm about COLAs; after all, what if Mom's solution was "Here's the same $2.50; try to find pennies from somewhere else to get that milk!"?

Spousal Benefits

We've talked about FRA, but another big Social Security decision is about spousal benefits.

If you or your spouse has a long stretch of zeros in your earnings history—perhaps if one of you stayed home for years, caring for children or sick relatives—you may want to consider filing for spousal benefits instead of filing on your own earnings history. A spousal benefit can be up to 50 percent of the primary wage earner's benefit at full retirement age.

To begin drawing a spousal benefit, you must be at least sixty-two years old, and the primary wage earner must have already filed for his or her benefit. While there are penalties for taking spousal benefits early (you could lose up to 67.5 percent of your check for filing at age sixty-two), you cannot earn credits for delaying.[35]

Like I said, the spousal benefit can be a big deal for those who don't have a very long pay history, but it's important to weigh your own earned benefits against the option of withdrawing based on a fraction of your spouse's benefits.

To look at how this could play out, let's use a hypothetical example of Mary Jane, who is sixty, and Peter, who is sixty-two.

---

[34] Social Security Administration. "Cost-Of-Living Adjustment (COLA) Information for 2018." https://www.ssa.gov/cola/.

[35] Social Security Administration. "Retirement Planner: Benefits For Your Spouse." https://www.ssa.gov/planners/retire/applying6.html.

Let's say that Peter's benefit at FRA, in his case sixty-six, would be $1,600. If Peter begins his benefits right now, four years before FRA, his monthly check will be $1,200. If Mary Jane begins taking spousal benefits in two years at the earliest date possible, her monthly benefits will be reduced by 67.5 percent, to $520 per month (remember, at FRA, the most she can qualify for is half of Peter's FRA benefit).

What if Peter and Mary Jane both wait until FRA? At sixty-six, Peter begins taking his full benefit of $1,600 a month. Two years later, when she reaches age sixty-six, Mary Jane will qualify for $800 a month. By waiting until FRA, the couple's monthly benefit goes from $1,720 to $2,400.

What if Peter delays until seventy to get his maximum possible benefit? For each year past FRA that he delays, his monthly benefits increase by 8 percent. This means that, at seventy, he could file for a monthly benefit of $2,112. However, delayed retirement credits do not affect spousal benefits, so as soon as Peter files at seventy, Mary Jane would also file (at age sixty-eight) for her maximum benefit of $800, so their highest possible combined monthly check is $2,912.[36]

When it comes to your Social Security benefits, you obviously will want to consider if a monthly check based on a fraction of your spouse's earnings will be comparable to or larger than your own earnings history.

I've thrown a lot of numbers at you to consider, like your FRA based on your year of birth, as well as the COLA and spousal benefits (and we haven't even gotten to taxes!), but here's another date to think about: January 2, 1954. What's important about that, you ask? For those born on or after that date, you can only make the choice to withdraw your benefits one way, one time. That means you will have to pick whether to take a spousal benefit or use your own earnings history, and

---

[36] Office of the Chief Actuary. Social Security Administration. "Social Security Benefits: Benefits for Spouses."
https://www.ssa.gov/OACT/quickcalc/spouse.html#calculator.

whichever one you choose will be the check you get every month for the duration of your retirement. However, if you were born BEFORE January 2, 1954, read on.

If you were born before January 2, 1954, you are eligible to change your benefit withdrawal strategy *even after you have begun withdrawals*. This means that you could have begun taking a spousal benefit at sixty or FRA while allowing the benefits based on your own earnings history to accrue.[37]

Let's look back to Mary Jane and Peter to see how this could theoretically work. We know that if they both file at FRA, Mary Jane will receive $800 a month on top of Peter's $1,600 benefit when she files. But what if her own earned credit at FRA was $700? When Mary Jane turns seventy, the monthly benefit based on her personal earnings will have grown from $700 to $924. At seventy, she could file to trade up her $800 monthly spousal benefit for a $924 monthly check. Remember, this only works for Mary Jane if she was born before January 2, 1954.

Divorced Spouses

There are a few considerations for those of us who have gone through a divorce. If you 1) were married for ten years or more *and* 2) have since been divorced for at least two years *and* 3) are unmarried *and* 4) your ex-spouse qualifies to begin Social Security, you qualify for a spousal benefit based on your ex-husband or ex-wife's earnings history at FRA. A divorced spousal benefit is different from the married spousal benefit in one way: You don't have to wait for your ex-spouse to file before you can file yourself.[38]

For instance, Charles and Moira were married for fifteen years before their divorce, when he was thirty-six and she was forty. Moira has been remarried for twenty years, and, although

---

[37] Social Security Administration. "Retirement Planner: Benefits For Your Spouse." https://www.ssa.gov/planners/retire/applying6.html.

[38] Social Security Administration. "Retirement Planner: If You Are Divorced." https://www.ssa.gov/planners/retire/divspouse.html.

Charles briefly remarried, his second marriage ended after a few years. Charles' benefits are largely calculated based on his many years of volunteering in schools, meaning his personal monthly benefit is close to zero.

Although Moira has deferred her retirement, opting to delay benefits until she is seventy, Charles can begin taking benefits calculated off of Moira's work history at FRA as early as sixty. However, he will also have the option of waiting until FRA to collect the maximum, or 50 percent of Moira's earned monthly benefit at her FRA.

Widowed Spouses

If your marriage ended with the death of your spouse, you might claim a benefit for your spouse's earned income as his or her widow/widower, called a survivor's benefit. Unlike a spousal benefit or divorced benefits, if your husband or wife dies, you are allowed to claim his or her full benefit. Also unlike spousal benefits, if you need to, you can begin taking income when you turn sixty. However, as with other benefit options, your monthly check will be permanently reduced for withdrawing benefits before FRA.

If your spouse began taking benefits before he or she died, you can't delay withdrawing your survivor's benefits to get delayed credits; the Social Security Administration says you can only get as much from a survivor's benefit as what your deceased spouse might have gotten, had he or she lived.[39]

Taxes, Taxes, Taxes

With Social Security, as with everything, it is important to consider taxes. It may be surprising, but your Social Security benefits are not tax-free. Despite having been taxed to accrue

---

[39] Social Security Administration. "Benefits Planner: Receiving Survivors Benefits Early."
https://www.ssa.gov/planners/survivors/survivorchartred.html.

those benefits in the first place, you may have to pay Uncle Sam income taxes on up to 85 percent of your Social Security.

The Social Security Administration figures these taxes using what they call the provisional income formula. Your provisional income formula differs from the adjusted gross income you use for your regular income taxes. Instead, to find out how much of your Social Security benefit is taxable, the Social Security Administration calculates it this way:

Provisional Income = Adjusted Gross Income + Nontaxable Interest + ½ of Social Security

See that piece about nontaxable interest? That generally means interest from government bonds and notes. It surprises many people that, although you may not pay taxes on those assets, their income will count against you when it comes to Social Security taxation.

Once you have figured out your provisional income (also called "combined income"), you can use the following chart to figure out your Social Security taxes.[40]

---

[40] Social Security Administration. "Benefits Planner: Income Taxes and Your Social Security Benefit." https://www.ssa.gov/planners/taxes.html.

Taxes on Social Security

Provisional Income = Adjusted Gross Income + Nontaxable Interest + ½ of Social Security

If you are ___ and your provisional income is___, then...		Uncle Sam will tax ___ of your Social Security
Single	Married, filing jointly	
Less than $25,000	Less than $32,000	0%
$25,000 to $34,000	$32,000 to $44,000	Up to 50%
More than $34,000	More than $44,000	Up to 85%

This is one more reason it may be to your advantage to work with a financial professional: He or she can take a look at your entire picture to make your overall retirement plan as tax efficient as possible—including your Social Security benefit.

Working and Social Security: The Earnings Test

If you haven't reached FRA, but you started your Social Security benefits and are still working, things get a little hairy.

Because you have started Social Security payments, the Social Security Administration will pay out your benefits (docked, of course, for what you could have gotten if you had waited to file until your FRA). Yet, because you are working, the organization must also withhold from your check to add to your benefits . . . which you are already collecting. See how this complicates matters?

To straighten the situation, the government has what is called the earnings test. For 2020, you can earn up to $18,240 without it affecting your Social Security check. But, for every $2 you earn past that amount, the Social Security Administration will withhold $1. The earnings test loosens in the year of your FRA; if you are reaching FRA in 2020, you can earn up to $48,600 before you run into the earnings test, and the government only withholds $1 for every $3 past that amount. The month you reach FRA, you are no longer subject to any earnings withholding. For instance, if you are still working and will turn sixty-six on December 28, 2020, you would only have to worry about the earnings test until December, and then you can ignore it entirely. Keep in mind, the money the government withholds from your Social Security benefits while you are working before FRA will be tacked back onto your benefits check after FRA.[41]

Social Security is an important part of all retirement plans. I tell my clients it should make up no more than 30 to 40 percent of your retirement income. About five or six years ago, many Social Security employees retired and along with them, a lifetime of knowledge. There are literally hundreds of strategies and the best one is going to be different for every person or couple. Unfortunately, the Social Security Administration does not offer suggestions as to the best strategy for you. They want you to apply for benefits online and make a decision. You have one time to get this decision right, good or bad, and there is no going back. As a part of my income planning service we look at what we believe are the best options available for each individual. We help you incorporate your strategy using the latest software to help ensure our clients receive the greatest benefit from Social Security.

---

[41] Social Security Administration. "Exempt Amounts Under the Earnings Test." https://www.ssa.gov/oact/cola/rtea.html

CHAPTER 9
401(k)s & IRAs

Have you heard? Today's retirement is not your dad's retirement. You see, back in the day, it was pretty common to work for one company for the vast majority of your career and then retire with a gold watch and a pension.

The gold watch was a symbol of the quality time you had put in at that company.

The pension was more than a symbol. Instead, it was a guarantee—as solid as your employer—that they would repay your hard work with a certain amount of income in your old age. Did you see that caveat there? Your pension's guarantee was *as solid as your employer*. The problem was, what if your employer went under?

Companies that failed couldn't pay their retired employees' pensions, leading to financial challenges for many. Beginning in 1974 with Congress' passage of the Employee Retirement Income Security Act, federal legislation and regulations aimed at protecting retirees were everywhere, including a relatively obscure section of the Internal Revenue Code, added in 1978. Section 401(k), to be specific.

IRC section 401, subsection k, created tax advantages for employer-sponsored financial products, even if the main contributor was the employee him or herself. Over the years, more employers took note, beginning an age of transition away from pensions and toward 401(k) plans. A 401(k) is a retirement account that has certain tax benefits and restrictions on the investments or other financial products inside of it.

Essentially, 401(k)s and their individual retirement account (IRA) counterparts are "wrappers" that provide tax benefits around other assets; typically, the assets that compose IRAs and 401(k)s are mutual funds, stock and bond mixes, and money market accounts. However, IRA and 401(k) contents are becoming more diverse these days, with some companies offering different kinds of annuity options within their plans.

Where pensions are defined-*benefit* plans, 401(k)s and their individual retirement account (IRA) counterparts are defined-*contribution* plans. The one-word change outlines the basic difference. Pensions spell out what you can expect to receive from the plan but not necessarily how much money it will take to fund those benefits. With 401(k)s, an employer sets a standard for how much they will contribute (if any), and you can be certain of what you are contributing, but there is no outline for what you can expect to receive in return for those contributions.

Employment looks very different these days. A 2018 survey by the Bureau of Labor Statistics determined U.S. workers stayed with their employers a median of about four years. Workers ages fifty-five to sixty-four had a little more staying power and were most likely to stay with their employer for about ten years.[42] Additionally, the outlook on the benefits front is different today, too. In 1979, 38 percent of workers had pensions. But 401(k)s are rising in number, with about 55 million American workers enrolled in a plan.[43]

A far cry from a pension and gold watch, wouldn't you say?

A corporate or government pension is a very desirable form of retirement, because a pension allows you to plan or map out

---

[42] Bureau of Labor Statistics. September 20, 2018. "Employee Tenure Summary." https://www.bls.gov/news.release/tenure.nr0.htm

[43] Investment Company Institute. December 31, 2018. "Frequently Asked Questions about 401(k) Plan Research." https://www.ici.org/policy/retirement/plan/401k/faqs_401k

your retirement by knowing in advance the source and amount of income you will have in addition to Social Security. A 401(k) or IRA alone cannot offer that advanced knowledge or peace of mind, as they can be subject to many variables, most especially stock market fluctuations. There is a big difference between income planning and income guessing. There are ways to mitigate these variables by taking a portion of your IRA or 401(k) and creating your personal pension.

If there is anything to learn from this paradigm shift, it's that you have to look out for you. Whether you have worked for a company for two years or twenty, you are still the one who has to look out for your own best interests. That holds doubly true when it comes to preparing for retirement. If you are one of the lucky ones who still has a pension, good for you. But for the rest of us, it is likely that a 401(k)—or possibly one of its nonprofit- or government-job counterparts, a 403(b) or 457 plan—is one of your biggest assets for retirement.

Some employers offer incentives to contribute to their company plans, like a company match. On that subject, I have one thing to say: DO IT! Nothing in life is free, as they say, but a company match on your retirement funds is about as close to free money as I think it gets. If you can make the minimum to qualify for your company's match at all, go for it.

Now, it's likely that during our working years, we mostly "set and forget" our 401(k) funding. Because it is tax-advantaged, your employer is taking money from your paycheck—before taxes—and putting it into your plan for you. Maybe you got to pick a selection of investments, or maybe your company only offers one choice of investment in your 401(k). But when you are ready to retire or move jobs, you have choices to make that require a little more thought and care.

When you are ready to part ways with your job, you have a few options:

- Leave the money where it is

- Take the cash (and pay income taxes and perhaps a 10 percent additional federal tax if you are younger than age 59 ½)
- Transfer the money to another employer plan (if the new plan allows)
- Roll the money over into a self-directed IRA

Now, these are just general options. You will have to decide, with the help of a financial professional registered to provide investment advice, what's right for you.

Remember what we said earlier about how we change jobs more often these days? That means you likely have a 401(k) with your current company, but you may also have a number of IRAs from other jobs.

When it comes to your retirement income, it's important to be able to pull together ALL of your assets, so you can examine what you have and where, and then decide what you will do with it.

Tax-Qualified, Tax-Preferred, Tax-Deferred ... Still TAXED

Financial media often cite IRAs and 401(k)s for their tax benefits. After all, with traditional plans, you put your money in, pre-tax, and it hopefully grows for years, even decades, untaxed. That's why these accounts are called tax-qualified or tax-deferred assets. They aren't TAX-FREE! Rarely does Uncle Sam allow business to go on without receiving his piece of the pie, and your retirement assets are no different. If you didn't pay taxes on the front end, you will pay taxes on the money you withdraw from these accounts in retirement. Don't get me wrong: This isn't an inherently bad thing, nor is it a good thing; it's just the way it is. It's important to understand, though, for the sake of planning ahead.

In retirement, many people assume they will be in a lower tax bracket. Are you planning to pare down your lifestyle in retirement? Perhaps you are, and perhaps you will have substantially less income in retirement. But many of my clients tell me they want to live life more or less the same as they always have. The money they would previously have spent on business attire or gas for their commute they now want to spend on hobbies and grandchildren. That's all fine, and for many of them, it is doable, but does it put them in a lower tax bracket? No.

Keep in mind, IRAs, 401(k)s, and their alternatives have a few limitations because of their special tax status. For one thing, the IRS sets limits on your contributions to these retirement accounts. If you are contributing to a 401(k) or an equivalent nonprofit or government plan, your annual contribution limit is $19,500 (as of 2020). If you are fifty or older, the IRS allows additional contributions, called catch-up contributions, of up to $6,500 on top of the regular limit of $19,500. For an IRA, the limit is $6,000, with a catch-up limit of an additional $1,000. [44]

Because their tax advantages come from their intended use for retirement income, withdrawing funds from these accounts before you turn 59 ½ can carry stiff penalties, with a few exceptions. In addition to fees your investment management company might charge, you will have to pay income tax AND a 10 percent federal tax penalty.

The 59 ½ rule for retirement accounts is incredibly important to remember, especially when you're young. Many millennials I see in my practice come in and, while they may be socking money away in their workplace retirement plan, that is often the *only* place they are saving. This could be problematic later because of the 59 ½ rule; what if you have an emergency?

---

[44] Troy Segal. Investopedia. January 17,2020. "What Are the Roth 401(k) Contribution Limits."
https://www.investopedia.com/ask/answers/102714/what-are-roth-401k-contibution-limits.asp

It is important to fund your retirement, but you need to have access to emergency funds. This can help you avoid breaking into your retirement accounts and incurring taxes and penalties as a result of the 59 ½ rule.

RMDs

Remember how we talked about the 401(k) or IRA being a "tax wrapper" for your funds? Well, eventually, Uncle Sam will want a bite of that candy bar. So another condition of these accounts is that, beginning at age seventy-two, the government requires you to withdraw a portion of your account, which the IRS calculates based on the size of your account and your estimated lifespan. This required minimum distribution—or RMD—is the government's assurance that it will, at some point, get some taxes from your earnings. Because you didn't pay taxes on the front end, you will now pay income taxes on whatever you withdraw, including your RMDs. Also, let me just remind you not to play chicken with the U.S. government; if you don't take your RMDs starting at seventy-two you will have to write a check to the IRS for 50 PERCENT of the amount of your missed RMDs.

If you don't need income from your retirement accounts, RMDs can seem like more of a tax burden than an income boon. While some people prefer to reinvest their RMDs, this comes with the possibility of additional taxation: You'll pay income taxes on your RMDs and then capital gains taxes on the growth of your investments. If you are legacy minded, there are other ways to use RMDs, many of which have tax benefits.

Permanent Life Insurance
One way to turn those pesky RMDs into a legacy is through permanent life insurance. If properly structured and you can qualify for it medically, these products avoid taxation and can pass on that sizeable death benefit to your beneficiaries as part of your general legacy plan.

ILIT

Another way to use RMDs toward your legacy is to work with an estate planning attorney to create an irrevocable life insurance trust (ILIT). This is basically a permanent life insurance policy within a trust. Because the trust is irrevocable, you would relinquish control of it, but, unlike with just a permanent life insurance policy, your death benefit won't count toward your taxable estate.

Annuities

Because annuities can be tax-deferred, funneling your RMDs into an annuity contract can be one way to further delay taxation while guaranteeing your income payments (either to you or your loved ones) later.

QCD

If you are charity-minded, you may use your RMDs toward a charitable organization, instead of using them for income. You must do this directly from your retirement account (you can't take the RMD check and *then* pay the charity) for your withdrawals to be qualified charitable distributions (QCDs), but this is one way of realizing some of the benefits of a charitable legacy during your own lifetime. You will not need to pay taxes on your QCDs, and they won't count toward your annual charitable tax deduction limit, plus you'll be able to see how the organization you are supporting uses your donations.

Taxes and Retirement

It's important to plan for RMDs to help mitigate the tax consequences. Congress is expected to raise taxes after December 31, 2025. Up until then, in effect, taxes are "on sale," so to speak. We know they will likely be going up after that date because Congress has told us so. We have until then to convert taxable IRAs into tax-efficient Roth IRAs and LIRPs at today's lower tax rates. By converting an IRA now, the potential tax savings for an individual with a qualified account that begins

RMDs at age seventy-two through ninety are significant. This can be a great strategy for individuals between fifty and sixty-five years of age. And you may not want to convert your IRAs in a single year. Consider spreading the tax consequences between now and December 31, 2025.

Roth

Since the Taxpayer Relief Act of 1997, there has been a different kind of retirement account available to the public: the Roth. Roth IRAs and Roth 401(k)s each differ from their traditional counterparts in one big way, which is that you pay your taxes on the front end. This means once your post-tax money is in the Roth account, as long as you follow the rules and limitations of that account, your distributions are truly tax-free. You won't pay income tax when you take withdrawals, so, in turn, you don't have to worry about RMDs. However, Roth accounts have the same limitations as traditional 401(k)s and IRAs when it comes to withdrawing money before age 59 ½. Also, the account needs to be open for at least five years in order for withdrawals to be tax free.

Taking Charge

As mentioned earlier, the 401(k) and IRA have largely replaced pensions, but they aren't an equal trade.

Pensions are employer-funded; the money feeding into them is money that wouldn't ever show up on your pay stub. Because 401(k)s are self-funded, you must actively and consciously save. This distinction has made a difference when it comes to funding retirement. According to one NerdWallet article, the "average" 401(k) balance for a person age sixty to sixty-nine is $198,600, but the *median*—the average if you look to the middle of the pack and don't include the super high or super low outliers—likely tells the full story. The median 401(k) balance for a person age sixty to sixty-nine is $63,000. The article also cites the general suggestion to aim, by age thirty, to have saved up an amount equal to 50 percent to 100 percent of your annual salary.[45] For some thirty-year-olds, saving half an annual salary by age thirty is more than some sixty-to-sixty-nine-year-olds have saved for their entire lives

There can be many reasons why people underfund their retirement plans, like being overwhelmed by the investment choices or taking withdrawals from IRAs when they leave an employer, but the reason at the top of the list is this: People simply aren't participating to begin with.

So, whether you use a 401(k) with an employer or an IRA alternative with a private company, separate from your workplace, the most important retirement savings decision you can make is to sock away your money somewhere in the first place.

---

[45] Arielle O'Shea. Nerd Wallet. January 24, 2019. "The Average 401(k) Balance by Age." https://www.nerdwallet.com/article/investing/the-average-401k-balance-by-age

CHAPTER 10

Annuities

In my practice, I offer my clients a variety of insurance products, all designed to help them reach their financial goals. You may be wondering: Why single out a single product in this book?

Well, while most of my clients have a pretty good understanding of business and finance, I sometimes find those who have the impression there must be magic involved. Like turning straw into gold, or like Jack and the Beanstalk going from a cow to a bean to a sack of gold, a harp and a goose that lays golden eggs, some people assume there is a magic finance wand we can wave to change years' worth of savings into a strategy for retirement income.

Yet, finances aren't magic; it takes lots of hard work and, typically, several financial products and strategies to pull together a complete retirement plan. Of all the financial products I work with, it seems people find none more mysterious than annuities. And, if I may say, even some of those who recognize the word "annuity" have a limited understanding of the product. So, in the interest of demystifying annuities, let me tell you a little about what an annuity is.

Generally speaking, insurance is a financial hedge against risk. Car owners buy auto insurance to protect their finances in case they injure someone, or someone injures them. Homeowners have house insurance to protect their finances in case of a fire, flood or another disaster. People also have life insurance to protect their finances in case of untimely death. Almost juxtaposed to life insurance, people have annuities in case of a long life; by providing consistent and reliable income payments, annuities can help with financial protection.

The basic premise of an annuity is that you, the annuitant, pay an insurance company some amount in exchange for their contractual guarantee that they will pay you income for a certain period of time. How that company pays you, for how long and how much are determined by the annuity contract you enter into with the insurance company.

How You Get Paid

There are two ways for an annuity contract to provide income: The first is through what is called annuitization, and the second is through the use of income riders. We'll get into income riders in a bit, but let's talk about annuitization. That nice, long word is, in my opinion, one reason annuities have a reputation for mystery and misinformation.

Annuitization

When someone "annuitizes" a contract, it is the point where he or she turns on the income stream. Once a contract has been annuitized, there is no going back. If the policyholder lives longer than the insurance company planned, the insurance company is still obligated to pay him or her, even if the payments end up being way more than the contract's actual value. If, however, the policyholder dies an untimely death, depending on the contract type, the insurance company may keep anything left of the money that funded the annuity—nothing would be paid out to the contract holder's survivors. You see where that could make some people balk?

At a high level, here's how it looks from the insurance company's side: Imagine the company has a "pie" of 10 people, who all buy contracts at the same time. In the beginning, 10 people receive income paid out by the company. A few, let's say three, die earlier on. Their remaining contract values are pooled back into the rest of the insurance company's pie. As the others age, they too die, many of them breaking even, with their pieces of the pie reaching zero around the time they pass away. One or two people even live well past the others, and, by the time they pass away, they have long since hit zero on the values of their contracts. The insurance company was still able to pay them their contractually agreed income using the money left in the pie, pooled from the two or three who passed away much earlier.

Now, I use this pie illustration as a way to show you the original concept of annuitization and how it works, from the perspectives of both an insurer and a contract holder. Modern annuities have so many bells and whistles that the picture I just described seems too simplified to do them justice, but it's important to at least have a basic concept of annuitization.

Riders

Remember what I said about bells and whistles? Modern annuities have a lot of different options these days, many in the form of riders that you can add to your contract for a fee—usually about 1 percent of the contract value per year. Each rider has its particularities, and the types of riders available will vary by the type of annuity contract purchased, but just to outline some of these little extras:

- Lifetime income rider: Contract guarantees you an enhanced income for life
- Death benefit rider: Contract pays an enhanced death benefit to your beneficiaries even if you have annuitized
- Return of premium rider: Guarantees that you (or your beneficiaries) will at least receive back the premium value of the annuity

- Long-term care rider: Provides a certain amount, sometimes as much as twice the principal value of the contract, to help pay for long-term care if the contract holder is moved to a nursing home or assisted living situation

This isn't an extensive look, and usually the riders have fancier names based on the issuing company, like Lorem Ipsum Insurance Company Income Preferred Bonus Fixed Index Annuity rider, but I just wanted to show you what some of the general options are in layman's terms.

Types of Annuities

Annuities break down into four basic types: immediate, variable, fixed, and fixed index.

Immediate

Immediate annuities are not terribly popular because they primarily rely on annuitization to provide income—you give the insurance company a lump sum upfront, and your payments begin immediately. Once you begin receiving income payments, the transaction is irreversible and you no longer have access to your money in a lump sum. When you die, any remaining contract value is forfeited to the insurance company.

All other annuity contract types are "deferred" contracts, meaning you fund your policy as a lump sum or over a period of years and you give it the opportunity to grow over time—sometimes years, sometimes decades.

Variable

A variable annuity is an insurance contract that has an investment component. It's sold by insurance companies, but only through someone who is registered to sell investment products. With a variable annuity contract, you are indirectly investing in the market through underlying mutual funds. This makes it a bit different from the other annuity contract types because it is the only contract in which your money is subject to losses as a result of market declines. Your contract value has a greater opportunity to grow, but it also stands to lose. Additionally, your contract's value will be subject to the underlying investment's fees and limitations—including capital gains taxes, management fees, etc. Once it is time for you to receive income from the contract, the insurance company will pay you a certain income, locked in at whatever your contract's value was.

I try to avoid variable annuities for those approaching retirement because of the market risk involved, as well as the potential for higher fees attached to these products.

Fixed

A traditional fixed annuity is pretty straightforward. You purchase a contract with a guaranteed interest rate and, when you are ready, the insurance company will make regular income payments to you at whatever payout rate your contract guarantees. Those payments will continue for the rest of your life and, if you choose, for the remainder of your spouse's life.

Fixed annuities don't have much in the way of upside potential, but many people like them for their guarantees (after all, if your Aunt May lived to be ninety-five, knowing you have a paycheck later in life can be a mental and financial safety net) as well as for their predictability. Unlike variable annuities, which are subject to market risk and might be up one year and down the next, you can pretty well calculate the value of your fixed annuity over your lifetime.

Fixed Index

To recap, variable annuities take on more risk to offer more possibilities to grow. Fixed annuities have less potential growth, but they protect your principal. In the last couple of decades, many insurance companies have begun offering fixed index annuities. Fixed index annuities offer greater growth potential than traditional fixed annuities but generally less than variable annuities. Like traditional fixed annuities, however, fixed index annuities are protected from downside market losses.

With fixed index annuities, instead of your contract value growing at a set interest rate like a traditional fixed annuity, it has the potential to grow within a range. Your contract value is credited interest based on the performance of an external market index like the S&P 500. You can't invest in the S&P 500 directly, but the insurance company will credit your annuity contract based on the S&P 500's gains each year, up to a limit such as a cap, spread or participation rate. For instance, if your contract caps your interest at 5 percent, then in a year that the S&P 500 gains 3 percent, your annuity value increases 3 percent. If the S&P 500 gains 35 percent, your annuity value gets a 5 percent interest bump. But since your money isn't actually invested in the market with a fixed index annuity, if the market nosedives (2000 and 2008, anyone?), you won't see any increase in your contract value. Conversely, there will also be no decrease in your contract value—no matter how badly the market performed, you won't lose any of the interest you were credited in previous years.

So, what if the S&P 500 shows a market loss of 30 percent? Your contract value isn't going anywhere (although your value will still be reduced by the cost of any additional benefits or riders you have selected). For those who are more interested in protection than growth potential, fixed index annuities can be an attractive option because, when the stock market has a long period of positive performance, a fixed index annuity will enjoy a conservative interest gain. And during stretches when the stock market is erratic, and stock values across the board take significant losses? Fixed index annuities won't lose anything from the stock market volatility.

One strategy that involves a fixed index annuity (FIA) is to use an index with a participation rate or spread. A cap on an index does just that. It limits upside opportunity. A 12 percent gain with a 5 percent cap means you get a credit of 5 percent. If you have a 70 perceent par rate and the index goes up 12 percent, your participation index credit is 8.4 percent. An index with a 1.5 percent spread would work this way. A 12 percent gain minus 1.5 percent spread equals index credit of 10.5 percent. In both examples you're not capping your potential gains. Remember with a capped, participating or spread strategy, you are protecting yourself against 100 percent of downside market risk.

Other Things to Know About Annuities

We just talked about the four different kinds of annuity contracts available, but all of them have some commonalities as annuities.

For all annuities, the contractual guarantees are only as strong as the insurance company that sells the product, which makes it important to thoroughly check the financial solvency and credit ratings of any company whose products you are considering.

Annuities are tax-deferred, meaning you don't have to pay taxes upfront and on interest earnings as the contract value grows. Instead, you will pay ordinary income taxes on your withdrawals. These are meant to be long-term products, so, similar to other tax-deferred or tax-advantaged products, if you begin taking withdrawals from your contract before age 59 ½, you may have to pay a 10 percent federal tax penalty. Also, while annuities are generally considered illiquid, most contracts allow you to withdraw up to 10 percent of your contract value every year, but more than that and you could incur penalties. Keep in mind, your withdrawals will deplete the accumulated cash value, death benefit and possibly the rider values of your contract.

An FIA can be a good solution for individuals who want to avoid or minimize stock market losses. They can be used to create an income stream or for accumulating money over a period of time.

According to the Social Security Administration, when a spouse (typically the husband) passes away, between 30-50 percent of that couple's income disappears as well. Quite often the husband's pension disappears, and the lower Social Security income check also disappears. An FIA can be set in place to make up for that couple's lost income in the event of a death. This way the surviving spouse does not have to change the quality of life they have grown accustomed to.

Annuities aren't for everyone, but it's important to understand them before saying "yea" or "nay" on whether they fit in your plan; otherwise you're not operating with complete information, wouldn't you agree? Regardless, you should talk to a financial professional who can help you understand annuities, help you dissect your particular financial needs and show you whether an annuity is appropriate for your retirement income plan.

CHAPTER 11

Estate & Legacy

In my practice, I devote a significant portion of my time to estate matters. That doesn't mean drawing up wills or trusts or putting together powers of attorney or anything like that. After all, I'm not an estate planning attorney. But I am a financial professional, and what part of the "estate" isn't affected by money matters?

I've included this chapter because I have seen people do it wrong. Clients, or clients' families, have come in after having had a death in the family and have found themselves in the middle of probate, or high taxes, or have discovered that something unforeseen (often long-term care) drained the estate.

Alternately, I have seen people do it right: clients or families who visit my office to talk about legacies and how to make them last, adult children who have room to grieve without an added burden of unintended costs, without stress from a family ruptured because of inadequate planning.

I will share some of those stories here, not to give specific advice (obviously you have unique circumstances and will need the help of an attorney to be sure your wishes are carried out), but to give you some things to think about and to underscore the importance of planning ahead.

You Can't Take It With You

When it comes to legacy and estate planning, the most important thing is to DO IT. I have heard people from clients to celebrities (national rap artist Snoop Dogg/Lion comes to mind) who say they aren't interested in what happens to their assets when they die because they'll be dead. That's certainly one way to look at it. But I think that's a very selfish way to go about things—we all have people and causes we care about, not to mention those who care about us. Even if the people we love don't *need* what we leave behind, they can still be fined or legally tied up in the probate process or burial costs if we don't plan for those. And that's not even considering what happens if you become incapacitated at some point while you are still alive. Having a plan in place can greatly reduce the stress of those responsibilities on your loved ones; it's just a loving thing to do.

Life insurance is an incredible benefit for loved ones. It's not only a tax-free benefit but can make up for lost income that a widow or widower may lose because of the loss of a spouse.

It is also an oustanding way to pass on assets to beneficiaries. A policy owner can have the death benefit paid out over a period of time, (twenty years) to asure the kids don't spend everything at once. As one client said "I want to protect my kids from themselves."

Documents

There are a few documents that lay the groundwork of legacy planning. You've probably heard of all or most of them, but I'd like to review what they are and how people commonly use them. These are all things you should talk about with an estate planning attorney to establish your legacy.

Powers of Attorney

A power of attorney is a document that gives someone the authority to act on your behalf, in your best interests. These come in handy in situations where you cannot be present (think, vacation where you get stuck in Canada) or, for durable powers of attorney, even when you are incapacitated (think, in a coma or coping with dementia).

It is important to have powers of attorney in place and to appoint someone you trust to act on your behalf in these matters. Have you ever heard of someone who was incapacitated after a car accident, whether from head trauma or being in a coma for weeks—sometimes months? Do you think their bills stopped coming due during that time? I like my phone company and my bank, but neither one is about to put a moratorium on sending me bills, particularly not for an extended and interminable period. A power of attorney, or POA, would have the authority to make sure your mortgage gets paid or cancel your cable while you are unable to.

You can have multiple POAs and require them to act jointly.
What this looks like: Do you think two heads are better than one? One man, Chris, greatly relied on his two sons' opinions for both his business and personal matters. He appointed both sons as joint POA, requiring both their signoffs for his medical and financial matters.

You can have multiple POAs who can act independently.
What this looks like: Irene had three children with whom she routinely stayed. They lived in different areas of the country, which she thought was an advantage; one month she might be hiking out West, the next she could enjoy the newest off-Broadway production and the next she could soak up some Southern sun. She named her three children as independently

authorized POAs so, if something happened, no matter where she was, the child closest could step in to act on her behalf.

You can have POAs who have different responsibilities.
What this looks like: Although Luke's friend Claire, a nurse, was his go-to and POA for health-related issues, financial matters usually made her nervous, so he appointed his good neighbor, Matt, as his POA in all of his financial and legal matters.

In addition to POAs, it may be helpful to have an advance medical directive. This is a document in which you have pre-decided what choices you would make about different health scenarios. An advance medical directive can help ease the burden for your medical POA and loved ones, particularly when it comes to end-of-life care.

Wills

Perhaps the most basic document of legacy planning, a will is a legal document wherein you outline your wishes for your estate. When it comes to your estate after your death, having a will is the foundation of your legacy. Without one, your loved ones are left behind, guessing what you would have wanted, and the court will largely split your assets according to whatever the state's defaults are. And maybe that's exactly what you wanted, as far as anyone knows, right? Because even if you told your nephew that he could have your car he's been driving, if it's not in writing, it still might go to the brother, sister, son or daughter to whom you aren't talking.

However, it may not be enough just to have a will. Even with a will, your assets will be subject to probate. Probate is what we call the state's process for determining a will's validity. A judge will go through your will to question if it is in conflict with state law, if it is the most up-to-date document, if you were mentally competent at the time it was in order, etc. For some, this is a quick, easily resolved process. For others, particularly if someone steps forward to contest the will, it may take years to settle, all the while subjecting their assets to court costs and attorney's fees.

One other undesirable piece of the probate process is that it is a public process. That means anyone can go to the courthouse, ask for copies of the case and find out your assets, as well as who is slated to receive what and who is disputing.

It's also important to remember that beneficiary lines trump wills. So, that large life insurance policy? What if, when you bought it fifteen years ago, you wrote your ex-husband's name on the beneficiary line? Even if you stipulate otherwise in your will, the company that holds your policy will pay out to your ex-spouse. Or, how about the thousands of dollars in your IRA you dedicated to "children" thirty years ago, but one of your children was killed in a car accident, leaving his wife and two toddlers behind? That IRA is going to transfer to your remaining children, with nothing for your daughter-in-law and grandchildren.

That may paint a grim portrait, but I can't underscore enough the importance of working with a skilled estate planning attorney to keep your will and beneficiary lines up to date as your life changes for the sake of your loved ones.

Consider this story. My son, Ben, had a friend whom he hadn't heard from for a couple of days. He went to his friend's house to check on him but despite his car being in the drieway, he didn't come to the door. He range the door bell, no answer. His friend was dead from a heart attack at age thirty-four. The death of this young man was truly tragic and unexpected. He had a family inheritance, and it was assumed his sister would receive everything, as he was a single man. He did have a will but his sister was not the beneficiary. Turned out, he was engaged about ten years prior and his wife-to-be at the time was his sole beneficiary on his paperwork. This young man had called off the wedding and had several relationships in the years since, but never updated his will. This story is not isolated, it happens frequently. It takes ten minutes to review a will and possibly avoid a lifetime of grief for your loved ones.

Trusts

Another piece of legacy planning to consider is the trust.

A trust is set up through an attorney and allows a third party, or trustee, to hold your assets and determine how they will pass to your beneficiaries. Many people are skeptical of trusts because they assume trusts are only appropriate for the fabulously wealthy.

However, a simple trust may only cost $1,000 to $2,500 in attorney's fees and can avoid both the expense and publicity of probate, provide a more immediate transfer of wealth, avoid some taxes, and provide you greater control over your legacy. [46]

For instance, if you want to set aside some funds for a grandchild's college education, you can make it a requirement that he or she enrolls in classes before your trust will dispense any funds. Like a will, beneficiary lines will override your trust conditions, so you must still keep insurance policies and other assets up to date.

Like any financial or legal consideration, there are many options these days beyond the yes/no of having a trust. For one thing, you will need to consider if you want your trust to be revocable (you can change the terms while you are alive) or irrevocable (can't be changed; you are no longer the "owner" of the contents). A brief note here about irrevocable trusts: Although they have significant and greater tax benefits, they are still subject to a Medicaid look-back period. This means, if you transfer your assets into an irrevocable trust in an attempt to shelter them from a Medicaid spend-down, you will be ineligible for Medicaid coverage for long-term care for five years. Yet, an irrevocable trust can avoid both probate and

---

[46] Regan Rondinelli-Haberek. 2020. LegalZoom. "What is the Average Cost to Prepare a Living Trust?" https://info.legalzoom.com/average-cost-prepare-living-trust-26932.html

estate taxes, and it can even protect assets from legal judgments against you.

Another thing to remember when it comes to trusts, in general, is that even if you have set up a trust, you must remember to fund it. In my thirty-five years' work, I've had numerous clients come to me, assuming they have protected their assets with a trust. When we talk about taxes and other pieces of their legacy, it turns out they never retitled any assets or changed any paperwork on the assets they wanted in the trust. So please remember, a trust is just fancy legal papers if you haven't followed through on retitling your assets.

Taxes

Although charitable contributions, trusts and other tax-efficient strategies can reduce your tax bill, it's unlikely that your estate will be passed on entirely tax-free. Yet, when it comes to building a legacy that can last for generations, taxes can be one of the biggest drains on the impact of your hard work.

For 2017, the federal estate exemption was $5.49 million per individual and $10.98 million for a married couple, with estates facing up to a 40 percent tax rate after that. In 2020, those limits increased to $11.58 million for individuals and $23.16 million for married couples, with the 40 percent top level gift and estate tax remaining the same. Currently, the new estate limits are set to increase with inflation until January 1, 2026, when they will "sunset" back to the inflation-adjusted 2017 limits.[47, 48] And that's not taking into account the

---

[47] Ashlea Ebeling. Forbes. December 21, 2018. "Final Tax Bill Includes Huge Estate Tax Win for the Rich: The $22.4 Million Exemption." https://www.forbes.com/sites/ashleaebeling/2017/12/21/final-tax-bill-includes-huge-estate-tax-win-for-the-rich-the-22-4-million-exemption/
[48] Ashlea Ebeling. Forbes. November 6, 2019. "IRS Announces Higher Estate And Gift Tax Limits For 2020."
https://www.forbes.com/sites/ashleaebeling/2019/11/06/irs-announces-higher-estate-and-gift-tax-limits-for-2020/#18b9e5652efb

various state regulations and taxes regarding estate and inheritance transfers.

Another "frequent flyer" on the general tax concern list: retirement accounts.

Your IRA or 401(k) can be a source of tax issues when you pass away. For one thing, taking funds from a sizeable account can trigger a large tax bill. However, if you leave the assets in the account, there are still required minimum distributions (RMDs), which will take effect even after you die. If you pass the account to your spouse, he or she can keep taking your RMDs as is, or your spouse can retitle the account in his or her name and receive RMDs based on his or her life expectancy. Remember, if you don't take your RMDs, the IRS will take up to 50 percent of whatever your required distribution was, plus you will still have to pay income taxes whenever you withdraw that money. Thanks to rules enacted in 2020, anyone who inherits your IRA, with few exceptions (your spouse, a beneficiary less than ten years younger, a disabled adult child, to name a few), will need to empty the account within ten years of your death.

Also—and this is a pretty big also—check with an attorney if you are considering putting your IRA or 401(k) in a trust. An improperly titled beneficiary form for the IRA could mean the difference of thousands of dollars of taxes. This is just one more reason to work with a financial professional, one who can strategically partner with an estate planning attorney to diligently check your decisions.

CHAPTER 12

Indexed Universal Life

My clients are not typically gamblers. A day in Vegas playing the roulette wheel is more likely to give them nightmares than it is to make them eager with dollar signs in their eyes. Many would rather work with guarantees than with stocks and risk-based products, so of course, that sometimes means turning more toward insurance. However, no one wants to see their nest egg lose traction from inflation. What does that mean? For some of them, it means turning to a product called indexed universal life insurance. If you've never heard of that before, I'm not surprised. This life insurance product isn't suitable for everyone, but I want to take a second to talk about it because, for the right person, it can be a significant product in their financial arsenal.

Insurance: The Basics

If you haven't been casting around in the life insurance pond much, then let's take a second to cover the basics. During our working lives, it's likely we have some kind of basic term life policy, either privately or through our employers. Term life insurance means an individual is protected for a certain period of time, usually ten to thirty years. It typically correlates to a certain amount of wages (if it's an employer's plan) or a coverage amount chosen by the individual (if it's a person's private insurance). At its most basic, term insurance covers funeral expenses or something of that nature. Oftentimes, people will take out more than this—for instance, families with a stay-at-home parent sometimes purchase policies based on the working parent's life to cover years of income, plus the mortgage, etc. Your premium for a term life policy will be based on things like your coverage limit, your age, your health and the term of the policy. The older you are, the more likely it is that you have health events or other issues that have made it more difficult to obtain term life insurance and the more expensive it is. Some consumers may see this as a disadvantage of term life insurance, because they pay into a policy for twenty years and then it reaches its "endowment"—the end of the contract term—and there are no additional benefits.

Permanent Insurance

Aside from the basic term life policies that many wage-earners hold, insurance companies also have permanent, or "cash value," policies. With a permanent insurance contract, your policy will typically remain in force as long as you continue to keep it funded. (There is an exception for whole life policies, which we'll get to later.) A permanent insurance contract has two pieces: the death benefit and cash value accumulation. Both are spelled out in your contract. As these products gained recognition, people began to realize that they had significant advantages when it came to taxes. I don't really want to get too technical, but it is really the technical details that make these policies so valuable to their owners. That bit about tax advantages makes permanent life insurance policies attractive to consumers because not only do they get an income tax-free death benefit for their beneficiaries, they may also be able to borrow against their policy, income tax free, if they end up needing the money.

For example, let's say Emma purchases a life insurance policy when she's thirty. She hates the idea of not having anything to show for her premiums over ten to twenty years, so she decides to use a permanent policy. Then, when she's close to fifty, her brother finds himself in dire straits. Emma wants to help, and she's been a diligent saver. The catch is that most of her money is in products like her 401(k) or an annuity. These may be fabulous products that are suitable for her needs, but her circumstance has just changed, and she's looking for ways to help her sibling without incurring significant tax penalties. But wait . . . she has that permanent life insurance policy! She can borrow any accumulated cash value against her policy, free of income taxes. So, let's say she borrows a few thousand dollars from her policy. She didn't have to pay taxes on any of it. She can pay it back into her policy at any time. Then, let's say Emma dies before she "settles up" her policy (pays back that loan). As long as she continued paying premium payments or otherwise kept her policy adequately funded until she died, then her beneficiaries will still receive a death benefit, minus the policy loan.

Are you with me so far? The big themes on properly structured permanent life insurance policies: tax-free death benefit, income tax-free withdrawals through policy loans, in force for as long as the premiums continue to be paid and a minimum rate of cash value accumulation that is guaranteed by the strength of the insurer.

Now, let's get a little deeper on the two basic categories of permanent insurance on the market: whole life policies and universal life policies.

Whole

The "basic" permanent insurance policy, whole life policies are a "what you see is what you get" prospect. With whole life, an actuary in a back office has calculated what a person your age with your intended death benefit coverage, your health history, your potential lifespan—and other minutia—should pay for a premium rate. Depending on how the insurer's rate tables are calculated, your whole life policy will "endow" at a certain age—ninety, one hundred, one hundred twenty, etc.—so there is the risk that you could outlive the policy, and the death benefit would pay out to you instead of your beneficiaries, which may create unplanned tax consequences. Nonetheless, to qualify for your whole life policy, you will complete a medical questionnaire and possibly a paramedical exam, and then, based on that information, an underwriter will place you in one of these actuarial categories to determine your premium rate. One benefit of whole life insurance is the insurance company will credit a certain amount back into the policy's cash value based on your contract's guaranteed rate. Some insurance companies may also pay a dividend back to policyholders at the company's discretion.

Take Emma from the preceding example, and let's consider if her permanent insurance policy was a whole life policy. When she first purchased the contract, the insurance agent would have been able to tell her what her locked-in premium rate would be. She would pay the same amount, year after year, to keep her contract in force. And she could also calculate her policy's minimum cash value to the penny.

Universal

If whole life is the basic permanent life insurance policy, universal is the "souped-up" model. It has numerous speeds, comes in many different colors and has more options, which also means it might take some extra time and research to thoroughly understand. But this means that if it's right for you, it can be even more custom and can be fine-tuned to your specific needs.

The big differences:
- Flexible premium
- Increasing policy costs

Let's start with those increasing policy costs. Basically, the internal cost to the insurance company of maintaining your policy will increase over time, similar to a term insurance policy. Remember how whole life policies have those actuaries in back offices calculating all of that and then determining a set rate for you to pay to cover it all? Well, with universal life, that's part of the flexible premium part. You can decide to pay a premium that will cover your future policy expenses, or you can decide to pay a premium that barely covers your current policy expenses, depending on your circumstances.

That is where these policies have gotten a bad rap in the past. If you purchase a policy and only ever pay the minimum premium required, your policy could end up losing value to the point that your premium no longer covers your policy's expenses, and then the policy would lapse. That's also why it's incredibly important to work with a financial professional you trust, who can shoot straight about whether this kind of product would be appropriate for you, and to make sure you fully understand all the details.

To go back to our example of Emma, though, here's how a well-set-up universal life policy could work: Emma, ever the diligent saver, would have paid well over the minimum premium every month. Every time she got a raise or payroll increase, she gave her universal life policy a pay increase. With the policy's contractual rate of interest, she actually had a substantial amount of cash value accumulated in the policy. That way, when she decided to borrow money against the policy to help her brother, she could even afford to decrease her monthly payments for a time, until she was back in a better financial position.

INDEXING

Now to the main event: INDEXED universal life, or IUL. Like any permanent insurance, an IUL policy will remain in force as long as you continue to pay premiums, and you can borrow against your policy's cash value, income tax-free. And IUL policies are, at their core, universal life policies with that flexible premium. So why all the buzz?

If you skim back through some of the other policy details, I covered the ability to withdraw the cash value of your policy without paying income taxes, even on the accumulation. Because of the index part of IULs, that accumulating cash value has the potential to accumulate a lot more. An index is a tool that measures the stock market, like the S&P 500, or the Dow. You can't invest directly in an index, it's just a sort of ruler. With an IUL policy, your policy can earn interest credits are based on an index, with what is called a "floor" and a "cap." That means that, if the market does well as of your policu anniversary, your contract will be credited interest on the cash accumulation based on whatever your policy's index is, up to the policy's cap. If the market has a bad year and the index shows negative gains, your account still gets credited whatever your contract floor is. So, for example, let's say your contract cap is 12.5 percent and the floor is 0 percent. If the market returns 20 percent, your contract value gets a 12.5 percent interest credit. The next year, the S&P 500 returns a negative 26 percent. The insurance company won't credit your policy anything, but you also won't see your policy value slip because of that negative performance (although policy charges and expenses will still be deducted from your policy). So, your policy won't lose value because of poor market conditions, but you can still stand to realize higher interest credits due to index gains. The following chart demonstrates how the IUL policy works, assuming you've selected the S&P 500. As you can see, because of the cap, the IUL doesn't have the sharp upticks of the index, but it also never goes down due to market losses.

The potential cash accumulation is a real draw here for people who want protection from market losses, potential growth and a death benefit for their beneficiaries. Many people also prefer to well fund their policies and borrow against their cash values to help provide supplemental retirement income.

WALL STREET & YOUR RETIREMENT | 111

Keep in mind that policy loans will reduce available cash values and death benefits and may cause the policy to lapse, and additional premium payments may be required to keep the policy in force.

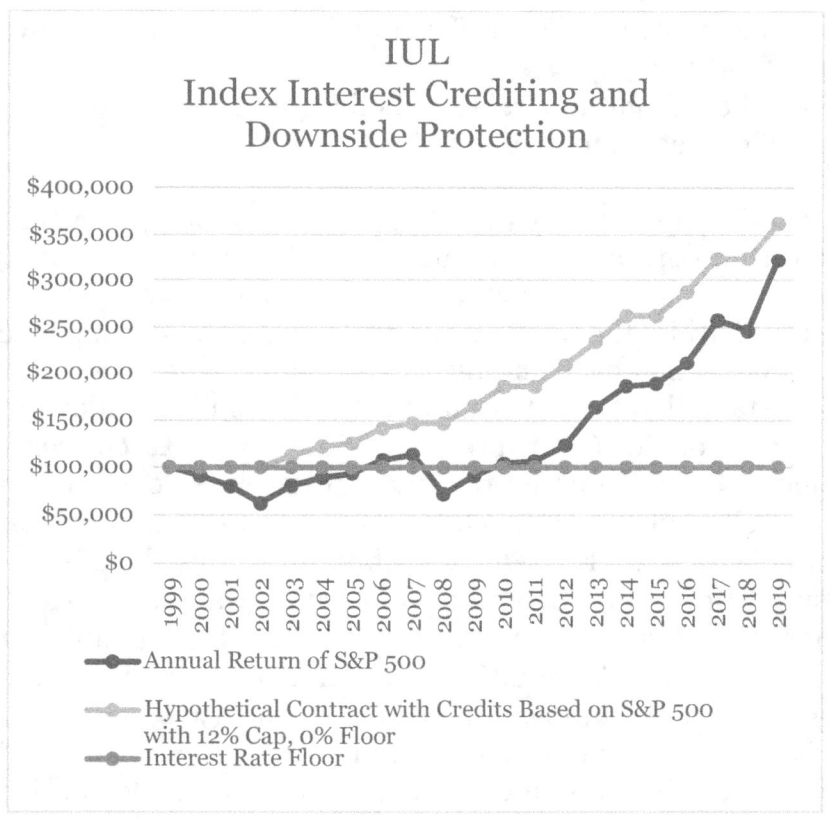

Preceding is a hypothetical illustration of the following:[49]
1. The top line, lightest in color, represents $100,000 used to purchase an IUL policy and allocated to an index interest crediting method tied to the performance of the

---

[49] Standard & Poor's®, S&P® and S&P 500® are registered trademarks of Standard & Poor's Financial Services LLC. S&P 500® returns are based on information obtained from Yahoo Finance GSPC Historical Prices and StandardandPoors.com

S&P 500 index. It assumes a hypothetical cap rate of 12.5 percent and an interest rate floor of 0 percent. The policy was initially purchased at $100,000, and, after the interest crediting period, is valued at $323,441.
2. The second, darkest line represents the S&P 500 index, including dividends. The initial $100,000 would now be worth $257,799.
3. The straight line represents the guaranteed interest rate floor, equal to $100,000.

Another opportunity that IUL presents is for a policyholder to overfund the policy cash value in the first five or 10 years and then potentially not have to pay any more money into the policy, letting the cash accumulation self-fund the policy. However, when overfunding an IUL policy, it is important to understand that the policy may become a modified endowment contract, or MEC, if premium payments exceed certain amounts specified under the Internal Revenue Code. This can happen if a policy has been funded too quickly in its early years. For policies that are MECs, distributions during the life of the insured, including loans, are fully taxable as income to the extent that there is a gain in the policy over the amount of net premiums paid. An additional 10 percent federal income tax may apply for withdrawals made prior to age 59 ½.

So, back to our friend, Emma. If her permanent life insurance policy was an IUL, what might that have looked like? Emma saves, paying well over the mandatory minimum of her IUL policy. For decades, the market does very well. Her policy accumulates a significant cash value. At some point, she stops paying as much in premium, or maybe she stops paying any premium from her own pocket at all, because her policy has enough in cash value that it is paying for its own expenses with the insurance company. Then, when her brother needs help, there is enough cash value stored in the policy. It's important to note that making withdrawals or taking policy loans from the policy may have an adverse effect. You may want to talk to your financial professional to re-evaluate your premium payment schedule.

If you're reeling just a bit, it's understandable. There's a lot going on with these policies. If you don't take the time to understand the basics of how they work, it's entirely possible to fall behind on premium payments and end up with a policy that lapses. Yet, if you understand the terms of your contract and are working with purpose, an IUL could be a powerful cog in the greater mechanics of your overall retirement strategy.

For those looking to minimize taxes and give yourself and even your beneficiaries flexibility, this financial tool can be very complimentary to your portfolio.

AFTERWORD
2020 and Beyond

A question often asked by clients is what do I think about the future and its opportunities.

This past summer my wife Debbie and I visited Austria, Prague and Italy. I asked the same questions of individuals that I am asked, including what do you invest in and how do you save for the future.

Regardless of the locations we visited and languages spoken the people were all the same. They have the same concerns, hope dreams and desire that you and I do. The consensus of individuals I spoke with was the average citizen does not understand the stock markets or trust their banking system.

This is interesting because we visited the worlds oldest Bank founded in 1472. Banca Monte dei Paschi di Siena is located in Siena, Italy. You would think if you had access to the world's oldest bank it would inspire confidence, in fact it was the opposite.

Italy's oldest bank, Banca Monte dei Paschi di Siena

Based upon our conversation(s), Italians love to invest in real estate and keep their savings under the mattress. They don't trust their banks because when the bank makes a bad investment decision the depositors are responsible and they can confiscate the deposit. This is known as a bail-in. In the United States our government bail-out the bank(s) and insures individual accounts as they are protected by FDIC Insurance.

In Austria there was a similar distrust of banks. The investment of choice seemed to be gold coins. In Prague they are just happy to now be participating in capitalism and out from under the financial oppression of communism. Their future is still evolving and most are just living from one week to the next.

So what does the future hold for these people and possibly our own country?

On November 14, 2018, Christine Lagarde, IMF Managing Director gave a presentation called, Winds of Change: The Case for New Digital Currency. In her presentation Ms. Lagarde walks through the history of money and various societies starting with the Chinese during the ninth century. She describes in her speech that today data is the *"new gold."*

Her speech identifies the pros and cons of this financial transformation of moving from cash to digital currency. Not just any digital currency but one that is issued by a central bank.

An example given in her speech is that purchases will be tracked and the impact of your personal choices could impact your credit score.

"Consider a simple example. Imagine that people purchasing beer and frozen pizza have higher mortgage defaults than citizens purchasing organic broccoli and spring water. What can you do if you have a craving for beer and pizza and do not want your credit score to drop? Today you pull out cash. And tomorrow? Would a privately owned payment system push you to the broccoli aisle?"

Let's be honest, broccoli and spring water is a healthier choice than pizza and beer. But the idea that a person's buying habits are monitored could influence a credit score is not a benefit of the new system in my opinion. What happened to freedom of choice?

From Ms. Lagarde's speech: *"This is not science fiction. Various central banks around the world are seriously considering these ideas, including Canada, China, Sweden and Uruguay. They are embracing change and new thinking-as indeed is the IMF."*

I personally believe these changes are inevitable. I would encourage everyone to take ten minutes and read the speech:

https://www.imf.org/en/News/Articles/2018/11/13/sp1114 18-winds-of-change-the-case-for-new-digital-currency

Change is an ever constant and I believe we need to move forward with faith, hope, and optimism. Faith being the most important as it is the foundation of confidence and peace.

Acknowledgments

Many thanks to all the ladies in my life who helped make this book possible. My beautiful wife Debra and office manager Denise—without your assistance, this dream of writing a book would not have become a reality. I would also like to thank Michelle Cooper and Juell Moulden, my compliance officers. And my account manager Julianne Yingling and the lady who oversaw the production of the book, Regina Stephenson. Ladies . . . Thank you, thank you, thank you!!!

RON ANNO
About the Author

Ron Anno began his career thirty-five years ago in the insurance business. Starting as a field salesman at United Insurance Companies Inc., he very quickly rose through the ranks to a senior manager and was recognized as No. 1 National Manager of the Year.

Ron was co-founder and eventually sold his interest in NT Securities, with offices in downtown Chicago at the Chicago Board of Trade. NT Securities serviced clients in over fifty different countries. He served on the board of directors and as a consultant to Fiji Trading Company for over seven years and served as president of S.C.O.T. Financial Services Inc. for over fourteen years. Ron has passed the Series 63 and 65 securities exams and is insurance licensed in Florida. He has written articles for *Kiplinger* and *Senior News* and conducted numerous radio interviews.

As a financial advisor, Ron takes a different approach to financial guidance by working, when possible, with his clients' attorneys and accountants to create tax-favorable investment and retirement plans.

"After more than thirty-five years in the business as a financial advisor, I've had an opportunity to see what works and most importantly what doesn't when it comes to creating a financial plan. My main focus when creating a plan is to help my clients achieve their financial goals of not outliving their money during retirement."

Ron lives in Sarasota, Florida with his wife, Debra. They have three adult children and two beautiful granddaughters.

www.ingramcontent.com/pod-product-compliance
Lightning Source LLC
Chambersburg PA
CBHW050007230526
45465CB00003BB/1297